THE GRACELESS FALL OF
ROBERT MUGABE

THE GRACELESS FALL OF
ROBERT MUGABE

THE END OF A DICTATOR'S REIGN

GEOFFREY NYAROTA

PENGUIN BOOKS

Published by Penguin Books
an imprint of Penguin Random House South Africa (Pty) Ltd
Reg. No. 1953/000441/07
The Estuaries No. 4, Oxbow Crescent, Century Avenue, Century City, 7441
PO Box 1144, Cape Town, 8000, South Africa
www.penguinrandomhouse.co.za

Penguin
Random House
South Africa

First published 2018

1 3 5 7 9 10 8 6 4 2

Publication © Penguin Random House 2018
Text © Geoffrey Nyarota 2018

Cover photograph © *The Herald*

PUBLISHER: Marlene Fryer
MANAGING EDITOR: Robert Plummer
EDITOR: Dane Wallace
PROOFREADER: Lisa Compton
COVER AND TEXT DESIGNER: Ryan Africa
TYPESETTER: Monique van den Berg
INDEXER: Sanet le Roux

Set in 11.5 pt on 16.5 pt Adobe Garamond

Printed and bound by **novus print**, a Novus Holdings company

MIX
Paper from
responsible sources
FSC
www.fsc.org   FSC® C022948

Penguin Random House is committed to a sustainable future for
our business, our readers and our planet. This book is made
from Forest Stewardship Council ® certified paper.

ISBN 978 1 77609 346 5 (print)
ISBN 978 1 77609 347 2 (ePub)

*This book is dedicated to the hundreds of thousands of law-abiding
and peace-loving citizens of Zimbabwe, who over the first thirty-seven
years of their country's independence endured adversity, penury and
injustice under the governance of the first prime minister and second
president of the Republic of Zimbabwe, Robert Gabriel Mugabe.
It is dedicated to the members of my own immediate family, who
suffered intolerable anguish because of my commitment to the
professional calling of journalism during the dictatorship of the
former president.*

Contents

Preface

On 22 November 2017, a day after President Robert Mugabe tendered his resignation from office, Penguin Random House South Africa asked if I would write a manuscript to capture the dramatic events surrounding the downfall of the man who had clung to the helm of power in Zimbabwe for thirty-seven years.

I was given a tight deadline to complete the manuscript, a task made more difficult by the reluctance of key figures to give their input. I had assumed that both President Mugabe and his spouse, the voluble First Lady Grace Mugabe, must be seized with a burning desire to present their own side of their great story.

Normally, I would have approached the president's official spokesman, George Charamba, for assistance, even though he did not have a track record of facilitating interviews with the president, except when arranging the ceremonial Robert Mugabe birthday interview with the Zimbabwe Broadcasting Corporation. Charamba had, however, just shifted allegiance, and is now the official spokesman of Mugabe's successor, President Emmerson Dambudzo Mnangagwa. To expect him to arrange any useful dialogue with the former president would most certainly have been an act of impudence.

At the time of Mugabe's downfall, an unlikely person had been portrayed as his constant guardian, mentor and advisor: Father

Fidelis Mukonori, S.J., an affable clergyman of the Catholic Church. I was aware that Father Mukonori had granted interviews to some foreign journalists, in which he spoke mainly of his own role in the negotiations between Mugabe and the military generals, leading to the former president's resignation. I telephoned and requested an interview with him and, hopefully, with the former head of state. Mukonori said I must submit a list of questions in writing, but when I did so, he did not respond. Further efforts to contact him by telephone were futile.

While I was waiting to hear from Father Mukonori I discovered that his memoir, *Man in the Middle*, had appeared in bookshops.

In the circumstances, *The Graceless Fall of Robert Mugabe* is based on my own observations as a journalist over the years and on research into the events around the presidency of Zimbabwe's controversial leader of nearly four decades.

My narrative is based on my examination of events as I saw them unfold from my privileged position as a reporter and a newspaper editor. While my book will not be the only chronicle of the events in question, it will be among the very first comprehensive documentations, crafted by one of the people with a vested interest in the events – the citizens of Zimbabwe. There will, no doubt, be a host of other accounts of the man who will remain one of Zimbabwe's greatest and most controversial leaders and the dynasty that he created over a period of four decades. It is my sincere hope that Zimbabwe will benefit, in the fullness of time, from a proliferation of narratives about Robert Mugabe.

This project could not have been accomplished without the able, willing and proficient assistance of a number of people. I am most grateful primarily to my editor, Advocate Muchadeyi Ashton

Masunda. A long-time friend of mine, he was the chairman and subsequently the chief executive officer of Associated Newspapers of Zimbabwe when I was founding editor-in-chief of its flagship newspaper, *The Daily News*, and he later became mayor of Harare. Masunda's two gifts, an elephantine memory and an exacting command of the English language, were an invaluable asset during the writing of this manuscript. I am indebted to my son, Julian Tafirenyika Nyarota, a wordsmith in his own right, who became my primary researcher, proofreader and fearless critic. I wish to extend my gratitude to Annie Musemburi-Musodza, my former personal assistant at *The Daily News*, who sacrificed her weekends to provide administrative services for the project.

I would also like to acknowledge the contribution of Dane Wallace, my editor at Penguin, who did sterling work editing the text and structuring the narrative. I am grateful to my publishers, Penguin Random House South Africa, for their sustained commitment to publishing my book and for their loyalty to me at a time when I was receiving a very raw deal from my own compatriots in Zimbabwe.

Above all, to my wife, Ursula Virginia, and to my children and grandchildren, I am eternally grateful for your moral support, understanding, patience and enduring faith in me, as well as for the endless errands you ran, often amidst hardship, to make the manuscript a reality.

GEOFFREY NYAROTA
HARARE, JUNE 2018

Abbreviations

AIPPA: Access to Information and Protection of Privacy Act
ANC: African National Congress
CIO: Central Intelligence Organisation
DRC: Democratic Republic of Congo
ESAP: Economic Structural Adjustment Programme
FRELIMO: Mozambique Liberation Front
G40: Generation 40
GNU: Government of National Unity
IMPI: Information and Media Panel of Inquiry
MDC: Movement for Democratic Change
MDC-T: Movement for Democratic Change – Tsvangirai
MP: Member of Parliament
NCA: National Constitutional Assembly
NDP: National Democratic Party
NGO: non-governmental organisation
PAC: Pan Africanist Congress
PF-ZAPU: Patriotic Front – Zimbabwe African People's Union
SABC: South African Broadcasting Corporation
SADC: Southern African Development Community
UANC: United African National Council
ZANLA: Zimbabwe African National Liberation Army
ZANU: Zimbabwe African National Union
ZANU-PF: Zimbabwe African National Union –
Patriotic Front

ZAPU: Zimbabwe African People's Union
ZBC: Zimbabwe Broadcasting Corporation
ZCTU: Zimbabwe Congress of Trade Unions
ZDF: Zimbabwe Defence Forces
ZDP: Zimbabwe Democratic Party
ZESA: Zimbabwe Electricity Supply Authority
ZIANA: Zimbabwe Inter-Africa News Agency
ZIPA: Zimbabwe People's Army
ZIPRA: Zimbabwe People's Revolutionary Army
ZNA: Zimbabwean National Army
ZNLWVA: Zimbabwe National Liberation
   War Veterans' Association
ZUM: Zimbabwe Unity Movement
ZUPO: Zimbabwe United People's Organisation

1

The nomadic intellectual

'Don't play make-believe Marxist games when you get home.
You have no Marxist party yet, so you can't impose Marxism.'
– President Samora Machel to Robert Mugabe, 1980

The day was Tuesday 14 November 2017. An abnormally long presidential motorcade sped north along Borrowdale Road from the city centre of Harare, Zimbabwe's capital. At the Helensvale Shopping Centre, it turned right into Crowhill Road as it continued towards the Blue Roof, President Robert Gabriel Mugabe's palatial official residence, deep in the heart of the upmarket Borrowdale Brooke neighbourhood.

As the president settled back in the plush interior of his black custom-built and heavily armoured Mercedes-Benz S-Class 600 limousine, designated ZIM 1, he had no inkling that his motorcade would never again race along this particular road on the twenty-minute journey between his Blue Roof residence and his office in Munhumutapa Building in the city. This white-brick building, an architectural relic of the country's colonial era, houses the Office of the President and Cabinet. It is located in the centre of Harare, on the south-eastern corner of the intersection of Samora Machel Avenue and Sam Nujoma Street, almost diagonally opposite the Reserve Bank of Zimbabwe.

I

President Mugabe had occupied this esteemed and increasingly powerful office continuously for thirty-seven years, much to the growing anger of many of the country's citizens, particularly those who were not supporters of his ruling Zimbabwe African National Union – Patriotic Front (ZANU-PF). Public resentment against the presidency had increased of late, as Mugabe and his wife, Grace Ntombizodwa Mugabe, had taken to regarding the country as virtually their personal property. For the first seven years of his reign, Mugabe had served as prime minister. Subsequently, for a total of thirty years, he was the president of the republic, commander-in-chief of the Zimbabwe Defence Forces (ZDF), president and first secretary of the ruling ZANU-PF and chancellor of all state universities.

For the Mugabe family, home was an exquisitely designed twenty-five-roomed palace, which the president had contracted a Serbian construction firm to build in 2003 in an outrageous display of wealth. It is said that the Chinese-style roof of the colossal building is clad with expensive midnight-blue tiles that were imported, fittingly, from Shanghai in China. The construction costs are said to have amounted to US$26 million. It was alleged that some of the funds came from ZANU-PF, while the *Daily News* reported in December 2000 that other funds were diverted from the construction of the new Harare International Airport.

Long after the nocturnal peace of that hot summer night on 14 November had enveloped the city, rather unusual sounds were heard by those residents of the north-western suburbs who were still awake. That included me, as I alternated between fighting to meet writing deadlines and communicating on WhatsApp with fellow Zimbabwean journalists in Harare as well as all over the diaspora, since many had emigrated to escape from the depredations unleashed on the media by the Mugabe regime, as spearheaded by the information minister at the time, Professor Jonathan Nathaniel Moyo.

It later transpired that the source of the unusual noise was a phalanx of military tanks. They had rolled into Harare along Lomagundi Road, the main throughway to the city of Chinhoyi 120 kilometres to the north and, beyond it, to Kariba and Chirundu on the mighty Zambezi River, which forms a boundary with the Republic of Zambia.

On arrival in Harare, the tanks sealed off Munhumutapa Building and the Parliament of Zimbabwe in the next block, situated between Kwame Nkrumah and Nelson Mandela avenues. Numerous tanks positioned themselves outside Police General Headquarters near the intersection of 7th Street and Josiah Tongogara Avenue, not far from the State House, the unoccupied official residence of the president of Zimbabwe, which they also surrounded. A number of tanks then proceeded further, in a north-easterly direction, following the route to the Blue Roof. Zimbabwe's First Family had effectively spurned the official State House and relocated to this luxurious dwelling upon its completion in 2007.

After driving past the Borrowdale Racecourse, some tanks veered to the right into Whitwell Road and then right again into Ridgeview North Road while proceeding in the direction of Pockets Hill, the headquarters of the national broadcaster, the Zimbabwe Broadcasting Corporation (ZBC), where they positioned themselves across the main entrance to the premises.

The remaining armoured vehicles proceeded further north to the Blue Roof, where they quickly neutralised the members of the Presidential Guard who were stationed at the massive property.

3

Through this manoeuvre, code-named Operation Restore Legacy, the military had taken control of Zimbabwe. The president and his First Lady were essentially prisoners inside their mansion. Early in the morning of 15 November, following the house arrest of the Mugabes the previous day, a top-ranking soldier, Major General Sibusiso Moyo, appeared on television. He denied on the state broadcaster that a coup had taken place. He stated that President Mugabe and his family were safe and sound and that their security was guaranteed. He also emphasised that the military was 'only targeting criminals around [Mugabe] who are committing crimes that are causing social and economic suffering in the country'.

Notwithstanding this assurance, a series of events unfolded over the next few days that all but forced President Mugabe to tender his resignation by letter. In terms of the Constitution of Zimbabwe, this was handed over to the Speaker of the House of Assembly, Advocate Jacob Francis Mudenda, on Tuesday afternoon of the following week.

The date was 21 November. Mugabe was exactly three months short of turning ninety-four years old, in what had been an uncommonly long and extraordinarily eventful life.

Born on 21 February 1924, he was the third of Bona Mugabe and Gabriel Matibili's six children. By many publicised accounts, Gabriel was an itinerant worker who originated, as many immigrant workers did in those days, from Nyasaland (now Malawi).

Raised in Kutama in the Zvimba Tribal Trust Lands, in what is today Mashonaland West, one of Zimbabwe's ten provinces, the young Robert began his education at the nearby Kutama Mission, a Jesuit institution. There, he proved to be a student of more than average aptitude under the tutelage of Father O'Hea, a Jesuit of

Irish origin. The priest described Mugabe as having 'an exceptional mind and heart'. Mugabe was said to have built a reputation for leading a life of solitude, being something of a devoted bookworm.

One of Mugabe's childhood friends was James Robert Dambaza Chikerema. Born a year after Mugabe, Chikerema was his maternal uncle, and the two grew up while herding cattle together in the village. Many years later, Chikerema was to say in an interview that he remembered his young nephew as displaying signs of childhood insecurity. He said that Robert was somewhat of a bully and a sore loser at any of the games that the young herders played out in the pastures. He said that when Robert felt cornered by the other boys, he would drive his cattle to a secluded part of the open grasslands and spend the rest of the day there by himself.

Chikerema cited this as an instance of the intolerance that plagued Mugabe throughout his long political career. To add posthumous salt to a lifetime injury, Mugabe failed to forgive Chikerema even in death, much as he failed to forgive his political mentor, the Reverend Ndabaningi Sithole, founding president of the Zimbabwe African National Union (ZANU). Had Mugabe not wrested power from him in 1975 following a rift within ZANU, it is possible that Sithole might have become the first prime minister of Zimbabwe.

Tellingly, Mugabe personally denied Sithole and Chikerema, both of whom were distinguished nationalists, a decent burial at the venerated National Heroes' Acre in Harare. Meanwhile, less prominent functionaries, such as Chenjerai 'Hitler' Hunzvi and Border Gezi, were buried with full military honours with Mugabe's endorsement. Both of these minor ZANU-PF politicians were in the forefront of wreaking violence on innocent and defenceless opposition activists.

Many who reached Mugabe's level of secondary education in those days became schoolteachers, the only job easily available to educated blacks. So it was that after six years of primary school, Mugabe was offered an opportunity by O'Hea to train as a schoolteacher. Armed with a diploma, Mugabe left Kutama in 1945 and joined the teaching staff of Dadaya Mission, founded by Sir Reginald Garfield Todd near the Midlands mining town of Shabani, now Zvishavane. Todd, a missionary from New Zealand of liberal political inclination, later became prime minister of Southern Rhodesia.

For nine years after leaving Kutama, Mugabe was a teacher in various schools. While teaching, he did not miss the opportunity to improve his own academic qualifications, making use of private study to acquire his matriculation certificate. He then decided to proceed to the prestigious Fort Hare University in South Africa. Situated in Alice in the Eastern Cape, this became a key institution of higher learning for black Africans across sub-Saharan Africa from 1916 to 1959. A new institution called the University College of Rhodesia and Nyasaland enrolled its first intake in Salisbury in 1957 and soon gained popularity with Rhodesian students over Fort Hare. Nevertheless, Fort Hare University, which offered a Western-style academic education, produced many students who became famous, especially in the field of politics.

These included Nelson Mandela, Robert Sobukwe, Oliver Tambo, Govan Mbeki, Mangosuthu Buthelezi, Can Themba and Dennis Brutus, all of South Africa. Seretse Khama of Botswana and Herbert Wiltshire Pfumaindini Chitepo and Dr Tichafa Samuel Parirenyatwa of Zimbabwe were also alumni of Fort Hare University. After graduating from Fort Hare, Dr Parirenyatwa studied medicine at the University of the Witwatersrand in Johannesburg.

Mugabe graduated in 1951 with a Bachelor of Arts degree in English and history. Subsequent study saw him amassing six more degrees, including a Bachelor of Education by correspondence in 1953.

Mugabe returned to teach in Southern Rhodesia from 1955 to 1958. Later, he crossed into Northern Rhodesia, where he became a lecturer at Chalimbana Teacher Training College. Thereafter, he relocated to West Africa and secured a position as a lecturer in the town of Takoradi in the newly independent country of Ghana. During this period, his thinking was heavily influenced by Marxist literature and by the prime minister of the first independent nation of sub-Saharan Africa, Kwame Nkrumah. Mugabe continued with his studies for a Bachelor of Science in economics, done by correspondence through the University of London. And in 1958, while teaching at St Mary's Teacher Training College, he completed that degree.

There in Takoradi, Mugabe met Sarah Sally Hayfron, whom he would later marry. She was to become the inaugural First Lady of Zimbabwe and was well respected, especially posthumously. Zimbabweans developed a tendency to appreciate the good qualities of Sally after she had passed away, especially when they compared her with Mugabe's second wife, Grace, who is widely blamed for causing the disintegration of his regime.

With Sally in tow, Mugabe returned to Southern Rhodesia in 1960 while on leave. He immediately got caught up in the country's nationalist politics against the settler regime. After he decided to remain in Zimbabwe and join the National Democratic Party (NDP) as secretary for publicity, he resigned from his job in Ghana. The NDP, however, was banned in September of that year. Mugabe then became a founding member of the Zimbabwe African People's

Union (ZAPU). The leader of the new party, Joshua Mqabuko Nyongolo Nkomo, and Mugabe were to become the leading lights of Zimbabwe's nationalist struggle, right into independence twenty years later.

Following a period of disaffection with Nkomo's leadership style and his desire to gain external support against the Rhodesian government instead of promoting a firmer policy to confront the settlers, Mugabe and others in the upper ranks of the party rebelled in August 1963 and formed ZANU, with Sithole as president and Mugabe as secretary-general. This new party shared the same Africanist philosophies as the Pan Africanist Congress (PAC) of South Africa, while Nkomo's ZAPU was aligned with South Africa's African National Congress (ANC). While the nationalists have tended to ascribe differences of ideology and strategy, such as Nkomo's unpopular decision that the party's leadership should be based outside the country in Tanzania, as the cause of the split, an underlying factor was that of ethnicity, which they could not openly admit. The split divided nationalist politics into two parties: ZAPU, which was a mainly Ndebele-based faction popular in the south-western regions of Rhodesia, and ZANU, which attracted a predominantly Shona following in the rest of the country.

The Zimbabwe People's Revolutionary Army (ZIPRA) and the Zimbabwe African National Liberation Army (ZANLA), the military wings of ZAPU and ZANU, attracted Ndebele and Shona recruits, respectively. A breakdown of the results of the first majority-rule general elections in 1980 reflected this ethnic dissonance. Following the 1963 split, the nationalists who remained in ZAPU renamed the party as the People's Caretaker Council following the ban of ZAPU.

But for all their revolutionary zeal, culminating in a very long period of political unrest, the two nationalist parties were both officially banned by the Rhodesian government on 26 August 1964. Mugabe and others in the leadership of the parties were arrested and imprisoned indeterminately.

Using his imprisonment to continue furthering his studies, Mugabe obtained a Bachelor of Laws and a Bachelor of Administration from the University of London. He also tutored fellow inmates.

Ten years later, in 1974, while he was studying for a Master of Laws degree, two major events occurred in Mugabe's political career. First, while in detention in Que Que Prison, he was selected to take over the leadership of ZANU. And later that year, a number of the detained nationalist leaders were released from prison in order for them to travel to Lusaka, Zambia, to attend a political conference.

Early in 1975, Mugabe seized this opportunity to escape from Rhodesia by crossing the border into Mozambique. He had been ordered by Sithole – who was still in charge at the time, although his power had diminished – to travel to Lusaka to attend the funeral of Herbert Chitepo, the ZANU chairperson who had perished there in a car bomb. In defiance of the order, however, Mugabe headed east. After fleeing from Salisbury under cover of darkness, Mugabe and fellow nationalist Edgar Zivanai Tekere stayed for three months with Chief Rekayi Tangwena of the Tangwena people in Nyanga in the eastern highlands of Manicaland Province. Then, accompanied by the chief, the two crossed the border along the Gairezi River and entered Mozambique's Manica Province.

Samora Machel, who had recently been inaugurated as president of Mozambique, is said to have barred Mugabe's entry into the country because of fears that he was an agent of Ian Smith, Rhodesia's prime minister. Machel himself had emerged from the Mozambique Liberation Front (FRELIMO) guerrilla war against Portugal. His view was that the future leader of Zimbabwe should emerge from the ranks of ZANLA, from among those who were waging the guerrilla war against the Smith regime, and certainly not from among politicians who were emerging after spending ten years in detention.

At this stage, the Frontline States – then consisting of Botswana, Tanzania and Zambia – were insistent that nationalist movements engaged against the Salisbury regime, namely ZAPU and ZANU, should unite their military wings, ZIPRA and ZANLA, to form the Zimbabwe People's Army (ZIPA) under the leadership of Rex Nhongo, the *nom de guerre* of Solomon Mujuru. I interviewed Wilfred Mhanda, one of the guerrilla leaders at the time, while working on the manuscript for my first book, *Against the Grain: Memoirs of a Zimbabwean Newsman*. Mhanda, whose *nom de guerre* was Dzinashe Machingura, said that ZANLA and ZIPRA were working together to formulate a new war strategy, and in January 1976 they resumed military operations as a united force.

Mhanda said that Machel had always supported ZANU and was unhappy with this development. He demanded that ZANU identify new leaders, and the names of Mugabe and Josiah Magama Tongogara, the ZANLA commander, were brought forward. Mhanda claimed that Machel was furious because he didn't trust Mugabe and knew that the guerrillas didn't trust Tongogara either.

By way of compromise, the guerrillas had settled for Mugabe without really knowing him, and with the greatest reluctance Machel also accepted him. But no sooner had Mugabe secured leadership of ZANU than he closed down all organisations that united the two guerrilla movements, such as ZIPA. He was concerned that a single united movement might end up under the leadership of Joshua Nkomo, who had become the most senior nationalist leader after the demise of Ndabaningi Sithole.

It was in those circumstances that Mugabe led the ZANU delegation to the Geneva Conference in October 1976. But Mugabe's actions had alienated some of the leaders in the guerrilla movement. Mhanda felt so disillusioned that he refused to be part of Mugabe's delegation to Switzerland. Unfortunately, Mhanda failed to appreciate that Mugabe would view Mhanda's action as a threat to his own position. Throughout his stay in Geneva, Mugabe is said to have agonised over what he viewed as Mhanda's treachery in refusing to join the ZANU delegation.

To aggravate the deteriorating situation, the guerrillas were losing confidence in Mugabe at a time when he was getting unprecedented international exposure as a result of the talks in Geneva, which nevertheless failed to achieve any tangible results for the nationalist cause. Ironically, Machel also threw his weight behind Mugabe, in the belief that Zimbabwe's independence was not far from being achieved.

The last thing that the Mozambican president wanted to do was to back the wrong horse in the race for the first president of Zimbabwe. The change in Machel's attitude was not lost on Mugabe on his return to Maputo from Geneva. He prevailed upon Machel to act without delay to prevent Mhanda and his allies from staging a military coup against him. The Mozambican president moved in and ordered the arrest of 600 senior guerrillas, including Mhanda and the rest of the ZANLA high command. On 19 January 1977, fifty of ZIPA's top commanders were arrested in Beira in Sofala

Province, where they were attending a conference to discuss the reintegration of political and military leaders who had been arrested in Zambia in the wake of Herbert Chitepo's assassination.

Among those held were Elias Hondo, James Nyikadzino, Bernard Manyadza (alias Parker Chipoyera), Dr Stanslaus Kaka Mudambo, Chrispen Mataire (alias David Todhlana) and Dr Augustus Mud-zingwa of ZIPRA. Also arrested were Happison Muchechetere (alias Harry Tanganeropa), who later became editor-in-chief of the Zimbabwe Inter-Africa News Agency (ZIANA) and director general of the ZBC, and Alexander Kanengoni, who also worked for the ZBC and wrote a column for *The Herald*.

According to Mhanda, he was initially not among those who were arrested. 'In fact Mugabe invited me to work with him,' he said. 'We met a day after the commanders were arrested and I was informed of the so-called charges against them. I strongly disputed the claims and protested against this wilful and wanton act of victimisation.

'The charges against the commanders were vague, to say the least. They were accused of straying from the party line – *kurasa gwara remusangano,* as they say in ZANU.'

Mhanda said that he refused to cooperate with Mugabe and his newly established Central Committee. 'That's how I ended up in prison, too,' he explained.

No specific charges were ever brought against the prisoners, and they were offered no opportunity to defend themselves. Mhanda said that the men were held in a basement of the abandoned Grande Hotel in Beira before being taken by road to Nampula Province, where they were locked up for a week. They were then airlifted to Pemba, the capital of Cabo Delgado Province, in the northern part of Mozambique. According to Mhanda, they were confined to their cells there for more than seven months. Finally, they were charged with plotting to overthrow ZANU's leadership.

'They appeared before some form of kangaroo court,' said Mhanda. 'My understanding is that Mugabe was the presiding officer, assisted by Tongogara, Tekere, Herbert Ushewokunze and Emmerson Mnangagwa, who had just joined them in Mozambique after living and working in Zambia since 1970.'

After completing his law studies at the University of Zambia, Mnangagwa had served his articles with a Lusaka law firm set up by Enoch Dumbutshena, who later became Zimbabwe's first indigenous chief justice. Mugabe had appointed Telford Georges as the first black chief justice of Zimbabwe, but Georges was of Caribbean origin.

According to Mhanda, 'Mnangagwa arrived in Maputo bearing impressive political credentials, despite not playing an active role in the liberation struggle during his time in Zambia. He had developed a close relationship with Mugabe in detention at Wha Wha Prison and was married to Tongogara's sister. He went to Maputo at Tongogara's request and was appointed security chief, working out of the military supremo's office. It was the perfect launch pad for his meteoric post-independence rise to minister of state security.'

Meanwhile, the ZANU rebels, whose ranks had been increased by the arrests of Mukudzei Mudzi, Rugare Gumbo (who would become ZANU's secretary for information after independence) and Henry Hamadziripi, all previously imprisoned by the Zambian authorities on suspicion of plotting to assassinate Herbert Chitepo, continued to languish in prison. Conditions were extremely harsh for people who were described by Mugabe as counter-revolutionaries.

'We were subjected to painful, cruel and inhuman conditions,' said Mhanda, who was a brilliant student when we had both attended Goromonzi High School and the University of Rhodesia, before he fled to Zambia to join the liberation struggle. 'We were allowed out of our cells only once every ten days to empty the single bucket in which we had to relieve ourselves.'

The prisoners were packed in cells like sardines and were forced to sleep naked on cold cement floors. President Julius Nyerere of Tanzania heard about the conditions in which the prisoners were being held and prevailed on Machel to relocate them to another camp where life was hard but more bearable. They were finally freed when Lord Carrington, the British foreign secretary who chaired the Lancaster House Conference that led to Zimbabwe's independence, insisted that all political prisoners be immediately released.

Mhanda and his fellow prisoners went back to Zimbabwe after the ceasefire that brought the war of liberation to an end. He said that they found Mugabe being treated on all sides as a great and magnanimous hero. Machel had tried to make the prisoners' return to Zimbabwe conditional on their joining ZANU-PF. Mhanda and twenty-six others refused – which meant that in the first week after independence, they were arrested again and spent ten days on a hunger strike before Nkomo, the ZAPU leader, intervened to secure their release.

While the ZANU rebels were being held in Cabo Delgado Province, progress was finally made in seeking a lasting solution to the Zimbabwean political impasse. An internal settlement between the Smith regime and internally based nationalist leaders had proved to be a woeful sham. The internal leaders in question were Bishop Abel Tendekayi Muzorewa of the United African National Council (UANC); the Reverend Ndabaningi Sithole of what had since become an internally based faction of ZANU; and Chief Jeremiah Chirau, a traditional leader, whose Zimbabwe United People's Organisation (ZUPO) had a negligible following.

Universal suffrage elections held in April 1979 had resulted in Muzorewa emerging as the first prime minister of a country whose double-barrelled name, Zimbabwe-Rhodesia, reflected the relentless duplicity of the Ian Smith regime. The Bush War raged on equally relentlessly.

Under the internal settlement, 28 out of 100 parliamentary seats were reserved for white citizens, who constituted only 4 per cent of the population and yet were assured of control over certain government ministries.

'The recent election in Rhodesia was nothing more than a gigantic confidence trick designed to foist on a cowed and indoctrinated black electorate a settlement and a constitution which were formulated without its consent and which are being implemented without its approval,' said Lord Chitnis of the British Liberal Party. He travelled to Harare as leader of a group of British observers to monitor the 1979 elections. He submitted his report, *Free and Fair? The 1979 Rhodesian Election*, to the British Parliamentary Human Rights Group, which published it. 'We cannot play our appointed role in this process and endorse this blatant attempt to perpetuate a fraud and justify a lie,' Chitnis stated.

Rejection of the internal settlement by both the international community and the Patriotic Front was wholesale. Despite offers of amnesty in terms of the settlement, guerrilla activity escalated. The Frontline States, with the support of Britain and the United States, stepped up pressure on Smith and Muzorewa to hold another constitutional conference to include the Patriotic Front.

In 1979, at the Commonwealth Summit held in Lusaka, Margaret Thatcher, the British prime minister, agreed to convene a constitutional conference. The Lancaster House Conference, which was chaired by Lord Carrington, was the culmination of this groundswell of condemnation of the internal settlement. The resultant agreement established a new constitution for Zimbabwe, with a ceasefire taking effect on 4 January 1980. During the conference, Tongogara, the charismatic ZANLA commander, was one of the towering figures of the deliberations on the Patriotic Front side. Lord Carrington described him as a moderating force during the talks. Jacob Chikuhwa recounts in *Zimbabwe: The End of the First Republic* that such was the influence of Tongogara that when Mugabe started to tell Lord Carrington to go to hell during a press conference, it was the ZANLA commander who leaned over and calmed the agitated ZANU leader.

During the month of January 1980, Mugabe and Nkomo returned from Maputo and Lusaka, respectively, to tumultuous welcomes in Harare.

Before Mugabe and his delegation departed from Maputo, however, their host, President Machel, placed a damper on their euphoric preparations for their return home by insisting that ZANU-PF adopt a moderate and pragmatic approach in drafting their election manifesto.

'Cut out the rhetoric,' Machel reportedly told Mugabe, 'because you will scare away the whites and you need them. You will face ruin if you force the whites to take flight. Don't try to imitate us. Don't play make-believe Marxist games when you get home. You have no Marxist party yet, so you can't impose Marxism. It's difficult enough in Mozambique and we are a Marxist party.'

While the tables were tilted heavily against ZANU-PF in March 1980, Mugabe secured an overwhelming victory in the British-supervised elections that were held in Zimbabwe. The elections were observed by Lord Soames, who flew in from London to be the last governor of Rhodesia. So it was that on 18 April 1980, Robert Mugabe became the first black prime minister and minister of defence of the newly independent country.

Sadly, Josiah Tongogara, the enigmatic commander of ZANLA and one of the leading voices of the Patriotic Front delegation at Lancaster House, perished in a horrific car accident on 26 December 1979. Six days after the signing ceremony in London, Tongogara was driving north from Maputo to Chimoio, the capital of Mozambique's Manica Province. His mission was to brief ZANLA guerrillas on the implications of the Lancaster House Agreement, especially the ceasefire.

After sacrificing so many of his years to the struggle against colonial rule in his country, Tongogara died a few weeks before he was due to return to Salisbury in what ZANLA guerrillas regarded as their moment of victory.

The ZANLA high command's political commissar, Josiah Tungamirai, said that he and the commander had been travelling in two vehicles on the night of the accident. According to Tungamirai, he was driving ahead of Tongogara's vehicle in the dark, at a time when Mozambique's roads were notorious for their appalling conditions. Tungamirai said that his vehicle drove past a military one that had been carelessly abandoned by the roadside. There were no warning signs in place. Shortly after, the headlights behind him suddenly disappeared from his rear-view mirror, forcing him to turn back to investigate. He found that the general's car had rammed into the stationary military vehicle, and Tongogara, who was a front-seat passenger, is said to have died in Tungamirai's arms.

I drove on that road north from Maputo to Xai-Xai, the capital of Gaza Province, seventeen years later in 1996, when I lived in exile in Maputo. Even then, the condition of the road was a test of nerves and endurance.

In *The Great Betrayal: The Memoirs of Ian Douglas Smith*, the last prime minister of colonial Rhodesia writes that Tongogara's 'own people' killed him and that Tongogara had disclosed to him at Lancaster House that he was under threat.

'I made a point of discussing his death with our police commissioner and head of Special Branch, and both assured me that Tongogara had been assassinated,' wrote Smith. A lesser author than the former prime minister of Rhodesia would certainly have been excoriated by book reviewers for making such an unsubstantiated claim.

In spite of all the various versions of this rumour, Mr K.J. Silke, the pathologist at Mashfords Funeral Home in Salisbury, dismissed the allegation of gunshot wounds on Tongogara's body as totally false. He was quoted in *Tongo*, a television documentary produced in 1982, as saying that he had personally examined the body. He said that the rumour of gunshot wounds was groundless and that his findings were consistent with road-accident injuries.

Ian Smith did not explain how his commissioner of police and head of the Special Branch had reached their conclusion that Tongogara had been assassinated, presumably on Mugabe's orders. Neither official had ventured anywhere near the scene of the accident, and their testimonies were tendered at a time when the Rhodesian security establishment was in overdrive in its efforts to demonise

Mugabe. But on the basis of this single uncorroborated assertion, the last prime minister of Rhodesia planted the seed of a rumour that was to haunt his successor's long reign.

The reading public of Zimbabwe gradually learnt to accept, as perfectly normal fare in their newspapers, headlines such as 'Mugabe invites ghost to dinner' and 'Mugabe haunted by Tongogara's ghost at State House for 6 months?'

In this way, suspicion and rumour marked the beginning of Mugabe's long seat in power. And they remained a permanent feature of his regime, alongside regular news of violence and corruption.

As events unfolded, Mugabe's reputation as a nationalist hero and liberator – as a leader equipped with a broad education to serve his country – would begin to change. And so would Zimbabwe's fortunes.

2

Return of a heroic figure

'Don't you boast about having been to war, Robert. You want to personalize the war but remember we went together to that war.'
— Edgar Tekere

Robert Mugabe arrived back in Salisbury from exile on 27 January 1980. This was three weeks after the ceasefire that brought to an end the hostilities that had ravaged the countryside, pitting the two guerrilla armies against the Rhodesian Security Forces.

Following the ceasefire agreement signed at Lancaster House on 21 December 1979, the ZANLA and ZIPRA fighters of the Patriotic Front who had been in the Bush War started to arrive back home around Christmas. They received a heroes' welcome as they made their way to one of the sixteen assembly points that had been established throughout the country to accommodate them. At these points, the returning guerrillas could report, disarm and return to civilian life. A total of 18 300 freedom fighters had converged on the assembly points nationwide by the deadline of 4 January 1980.

While the ZANLA army of Mugabe's ZANU-PF had not scored a decisive victory against the Rhodesian Security Forces, Mugabe still arrived in Harare as a triumphant hero among the majority of the black people of Zimbabwe. Most of those who welcomed him had never set eyes on Mugabe before. But his reputation had preceded him. The ZANU leader was a man who was loved and hated in equal measure along racial lines. The Africans adored him, while the white population hated him with a passion fuelled by the rabid propaganda of Ian Smith's Rhodesian Front regime.

Compounding the issue, according to the British newspaper *The Guardian*, was the fact that Mugabe had told a press conference in Geneva in October 1976 that 'none of the white exploiters will be allowed to keep an acre of land in Zimbabwe'.

It was statements such as this, as well as the propaganda spewed out by media outlets that were not allowed to report positively on foreign-based nationalist organisations and their leaders, that had caused white Rhodesians to fear Mugabe. Meanwhile, the same propaganda had elevated him into something of an enigma and a national hero in the eyes of the black population because of his perceived determination to fight oppression and racism.

While the two foreign-based nationalist parties had presented a united front at the Lancaster House Conference, on their return to Rhodesia after signing the agreement, ZANU-PF had surprised its ally by announcing a decision to embark on a separate campaign ahead of the forthcoming elections. This was a shrewd strategy by Mugabe, as ZANU-PF's decisive electoral victory was soon to prove. The rivalry between ZANU and ZAPU was deep-seated, and throughout the years of politicising the rural population, the ZANLA guerrillas had always campaigned for ZANU and Mugabe, while denouncing Ian Smith and, occasionally, Joshua Nkomo. The unity forged at Lancaster House had been one of convenience. Mugabe had always viewed Nkomo with suspicion, the rivalry between the two nationalist parties being reinforced by the fact that they were based in two different countries, Zambia and Mozambique. Even their liberation armies, ZIPRA and ZANLA, had largely operated in separate territories inside Rhodesia.

It was widely said that a cause of misunderstanding between Mugabe and Tongogara, the ZANLA military commander, was that the latter supported the forging of a lasting unity between ZAPU and ZANU, whereas Mugabe was opposed to such a permanent alliance. It is for this reason that Tongogara's death soon after the Lancaster House Conference has been viewed with suspicion by some observers. In their opinion, the incident was a strategic move by Mugabe to pre-empt a liaison between Tongogara and Nkomo.

It was this fear of being overshadowed by Nkomo that had resulted in Mugabe nullifying the ZIPA alliance of ZANLA and ZIPRA back in 1976. ZANU-PF's decision to mount a stand-alone election campaign upon its return to Rhodesia after Lancaster House was therefore no surprise.

Joshua Nkomo was the first of the Patriotic Front leaders to return home, flying back to a tumultuous welcome in Salisbury on 13 January 1980, after three years in exile. He addressed a rally in Highfield township's famous Zimbabwe Grounds, with an estimated attendance of 150 000 people.

Mugabe's return home two weeks later, after almost five years in exile, was an even more awe-inspiring event. His homecoming rally on 27 January 1980 attracted a mammoth crowd, of a magnitude never previously witnessed in Salisbury. Journalists, including the foreign press, who had portrayed Mugabe in very negative terms, grudgingly estimated that the crowd had more than 200 000 ecstatic supporters. This far exceeded the number of attendees at the rallies organised by the other nationalist parties that were participating in the following month's general elections.

The rally was organised at the same grounds used by Nkomo, not far away from the house that had been Mugabe's original humble home in the Canaan section of the sprawling township. Highfield was the bedrock of African nationalist politics in what was then Salisbury. The rally reinforced the perception that ZANU-PF was in the forefront of the electoral race.

The crowd at Mugabe's rally would perhaps have even been doubled if the Rhodesian Security Forces had not stopped people from outside Harare from attending. It is my view that thousands of Zimbabweans could have turned out twice at Zimbabwe Grounds. First, they might have come to welcome the return of Father Zimbabwe, as Joshua Nkomo was fondly called, merely out of respect and, possibly, out of curiosity to see the first nationalist leader to return home. Then, the same people could have gathered again at the same venue two weeks later, this time to welcome the enigmatic Mugabe, the leader of the much-feared ZANU. This would explain the dismal performance of ZAPU in Salisbury and elsewhere outside Matabeleland when the electorate went to the polls.

That day, 27 January 1980, in the packed Zimbabwe Grounds, Robert Mugabe transformed from a hated and much-maligned subject of rumour and speculation into one poised to become a political legend.

Mugabe must have been overwhelmed by the huge turnout of people who came to welcome him. I believe that the seeds of his subsequent delusions of grandeur and his desire to exercise perpetual power were planted in his mind on that Sunday afternoon. Similarly, this is when any fledgling ideas about the establishment of a one-party state in Zimbabwe must have been reinforced. Former ZANU-PF secretary-general Edgar Tekere was to go on record many years later with the comment that the idea of a one-party state had never been on the party's agenda in Maputo during the liberation struggle. 'Experience in Africa has shown that it brought the evils of nepotism, corruption and inefficiency,' he explained.

On the morning of Mugabe's rally, ZANU-PF supporters arrived at Zimbabwe Grounds on foot, by bicycle, in private cars, on lorries and in buses from every nook and cranny of Harare in order to welcome the leader who had spearheaded the guerrilla war from Mozambique. There was wild applause when Mugabe stood up and punched the air with his fist, and the audience responded uproariously as he chanted his party's slogans.

I covered the rally for the now defunct weekly *National Observer,* a sister paper to *The Herald.* Speaking mostly in his native Shona, Mugabe told the audience that the need for land was the deepest of all the grievances among the people of Zimbabwe.

But Mugabe was placatory. He said that there would be no more injustice based on race and colour. While seeking to pacify the white population, whose major concern was the expropriation of land, Mugabe said, 'We will not seize land from anyone who has use for it. Farmers who are able to be productive and prove useful to society will find us cooperative.' Then, speaking in English, as if in direct appeal to white Rhodesians, Mugabe said, 'Stay with us, please remain in this country and constitute a nation based on national unity.'

The propaganda of Ian Smith's Rhodesian Front had portrayed Mugabe as a communist ogre who was bent on introducing a socialist economy that would entail the expropriation of land and private, mostly white-owned, companies. These were the backbone of the Rhodesian economy, which was in fact currently thriving, despite the existence of sanctions imposed by the United Nations.

To address these widespread fears, Mugabe said that in other areas of the economy, he would 'try to leave things as they are'. This rather tenuous olive branch failed, however, to dissuade thousands of whites from leaving the country.

In contrast, Mugabe had stronger words about Britain. He accused the British governor, Lord Soames, of manipulating the political situation against ZANU-PF.

The most prominent of the nationalist leaders vying for election as the first prime minister of the independent Republic of Zimbabwe were Bishop Abel Muzorewa of the internally based UANC; Robert Mugabe of ZANU-PF, which had been based in Mozambique; and Joshua Nkomo of the Zambian-based PF-ZAPU. Muzorewa had been prime minister of Zimbabwe-Rhodesia since the discredited and ill-fated Internal Settlement of 1979.

In the eyes of many observers, especially those familiar with the details of the war of liberation, Mugabe was the most popular of the nationalist leaders, especially in most of the countryside, where ZANLA had operated for many years before the Lancaster House Conference.

In her book *Re-living the Second Chimurenga: Memories from Zimbabwe's Liberation Struggle*, author Fay Chung states: 'To win the hearts and minds of the people, ZANLA had to be a politicized army that identified with the aspirations of the people. This was the lesson of the relatively unsuccessful years of the 1960s when local people would betray the guerillas to the colonial authorities. ZANLA began to build up a cadre of political commissars whose weapons were not the arms of war, but concepts, values and ideology.'

But the Rhodesian government, through its industrious propaganda machinery, battled to create the impression that Muzorewa was the presidential candidate most favoured by the electorate. Nancy

Mitchell, a professor of history at North Carolina State University, claimed in her book *Jimmy Carter in Africa* that the Carter administration methodically sought a buy-in from all parties – including, crucially, from the top three Rhodesian independence-movement leaders: Muzorewa, Nkomo and Mugabe.

Mitchell stated: 'Mugabe was in many ways the dark horse of the three. Muzorewa, a Methodist bishop, had studied in the United States and was lionized by conservatives like Senator Jesse Helms [Republican – North Carolina]. Nkomo was a *bon vivant* who travelled the world seeking funds, networking and living the good life. The British Foreign Office favoured him. Mugabe, on the other hand, was an ascetic intellectual who eschewed the backslapping that fostered friendships in the West.'

It was the enigmatic, principled and hard-line qualities of Mugabe, as well as his perceived potential to bring the drawn-out guerrilla war to a close, that endeared him to the majority of the black population. While serving as prime minister, Muzorewa had failed dismally to bring the war to an end or to bring any meaningful change to the lives of most of the country's citizens.

From June 1979, when he assumed office, Muzorewa's Zimbabwe-Rhodesia had failed to win international recognition. As a result, the country had been taken back into the hands of Britain, in terms of the Lancaster House Agreement, to facilitate a transition. While Muzorewa initially campaigned vigorously, attendance at UANC rallies continued to deteriorate. I covered a UANC rally in Que Que a week before the campaign deadline. Less than 100 supporters were in attendance, suggesting that the show was over for Muzorewa. Nevertheless, the media continued to cast him in the mould of a front-runner.

As for Nkomo, he had been relegated in recent years to effectively being the leader of an ethnically defined political organisation. Indeed, the election results reinforced this perception. Of the twenty seats won by ZAPU, seventeen were in Matabeleland. The Rhodesian government and its foreign backers, South Africa in particular, were petrified of a ZANU-PF victory and had hoped that Mugabe's party would not gain an outright majority. This outcome would pave the way for Nkomo, Smith and Muzorewa to form a coalition government.

And as for Mugabe's childhood friend James Chikerema's Zimbabwe Democratic Party (ZDP) and the original ZANU party of his former political mentor the Reverend Sithole, not a single parliamentary seat was secured between them.

Two weeks after Mugabe addressed the Highfield rally, he narrowly escaped possible death when eighty pounds of remote-controlled explosives were detonated under the convoy of cars taking him to Fort Victoria Airport. The explosives, set in a large drainage pipe under the tarmac road, were detonated from about ninety feet away. Mugabe had just addressed a well-attended rally in the town.

This was the second attempt on Mugabe's life since his triumphant return. A grenade had been thrown at his home in Salisbury the previous week.

Five ZANU-PF supporters were rushed to hospital for treatment of minor injuries and shock, the police said. 'It's a miracle anyone is alive,' a witness was reported as saying. He estimated that the hole created by the blast on the surface of the road was ten feet deep and thirty feet wide.

No arrests were reportedly made, although a police helicopter was seen hovering over the scene within minutes of the incident. Mugabe was forced to cancel a rally and a press conference that had been scheduled at the Great Zimbabwe Monument nearby.

The attempts on Mugabe's life appear merely to have enhanced his popular appeal.

Meanwhile, the British governor, Lord Soames, was reported as having urged the police to 'pursue the investigation with all speed and vigour'. Speaking through a spokesperson, he said that he was 'shocked and horrified at the attempt on Mugabe's life'.

In a separate action that day, Lord Soames took punitive action against Enos Mzombi Nkala, a senior ZANU-PF official from Matabeleland and one of the party's parliamentary candidates. Nkala had allegedly made public statements to the effect that the war would resume if ZANU-PF did not win the forthcoming elections. As a result, he was prohibited from attending any public campaign functions and from canvassing for votes in any way.

While Lord Soames insisted that his action was taken to halt widespread voter intimidation, Mugabe told a press conference that he feared the measures were designed to tip the scales in favour of ZANU-PF's opponents.

Mugabe told his supporters that he had warned Lord Soames that if he used his powers to ban ZANU-PF from participating in the election, then ZANU-PF would hold itself absolved from its commitment to the letter and spirit of the Lancaster House Agreement. 'He cannot have it both ways,' fumed Mugabe, 'ban us and expect us to be committed to a ceasefire. I am saying Lord Soames must choose. Is it war or peace?'

Going into the elections, ZANU-PF had presented to the electorate a moderate manifesto that bore little resemblance to the party's professed alliance with communist China. The party complained bitterly to Lord Soames, however, about an alleged official bias against it. Meanwhile, the registrar general of elections refused to incorporate the party's intended logo on the ballot papers, saying that it contained the image of an AK-47 rifle, which he considered detrimental to public order.

Throughout Mashonaland, Manicaland, Masvingo and most of Midlands Province – that is, all provinces except for Matabeleland – the rural populace immediately took to mock-flapping of their folded arms at every available opportunity as if they were wings, in the fashion of the cockerel, the new symbol of ZANU-PF.

Meanwhile, ZANU-PF posters were confiscated if they were considered by the registrar general to be inflammatory. The police arrested many party activists and some candidates. On his part, Lord Soames accused ZANU-PF of intimidating voters in twenty-three of Rhodesia's fifty-six districts.

On 4 March 1980, the election results were announced. The results confounded Lord Soames, the government and elements of the foreign press, as well as other detractors of Mugabe and ZANU-PF. There was jubilation in the ZANU-PF camp. The party had swept the polls by winning fifty-seven of the eighty common roll seats. Mugabe had secured victory by a convincing margin, receiving 1 668 992 of the 2 702 275 ballots cast, and was elected to lead the first government of Zimbabwe as prime minister.

That Mugabe would secure such a massive victory was never in doubt to those who were familiar with the political situation in the rural areas, where ZANLA guerrillas had consistently campaigned for ZANU during the Bush War. Foreign journalists, including so-called war correspondents, hardly ever ventured into the Rhodesian countryside, the theatre of war they were covering. Instead, they relied heavily on releases from the Ministry of Information and the military's Combined Operations. Far from seeking to inform the public truthfully or accurately, both sources of information were primarily designed to paint a favourable picture of the Rhodesian Security Forces' operations, while seeking to discredit or denigrate the guerrilla armies. The world was influenced accordingly, with shocking consequences when the election results were announced.

On 18 April 1980, Southern Rhodesia, the original name that Zimbabwe-Rhodesia had reverted to after the Lancaster House Agreement, finally gained total independence from Britain to become the fully fledged Republic of Zimbabwe. In a celebratory mood, thousands of Zimbabweans thronged Rufaro Stadium in the then African township of Harare, now Mbare, to witness Mugabe being sworn in as prime minister. Prince Charles, the heir to the British throne, watched sombrely as the British flag, the Union Jack, came down for the last time, to be replaced by the brand-new flag of the brand-new nation. As Zimbabweans celebrated independence, emerging reggae star Bob Marley performed his hit song 'Zimbabwe'.

Since then, 18 April has been celebrated as Zimbabwe's Independence Day, when the people of Zimbabwe commemorate the long, arduous and bloodstained struggle for their country's autonomy. In the early days of independence, the celebrations attracted thousands of revellers to functions held throughout the country, where the highlight was a reading of the president's speech. That day, 18 April 1980, became a high point of Mugabe's long political career. He spoke of turning swords into ploughshares, of reconstructing the war-torn land, and of restoring international confidence and internal stability. 'Let us forgive and forget,' he said. 'Let us join hands in a new amity.'

The conciliatory tone of Mugabe's much-acclaimed policy of national reconciliation struck the right chord both at home, especially among the white population, and abroad, among key Western governments and prospective investors. Mugabe's status as a hero of Zimbabwe's liberation was reinforced, while he became a political leader of international repute, being wined and dined in Western capitals, where he was showered with accolades.

The US provided the new nation with a three-year aid package that totalled US$25 million. The UK, the outgoing colonial power, financed a land-reform programme and provided military advisers to facilitate the integration of the guerrilla armies and old Rhodesian Security Forces into a new Zimbabwean National Army (ZNA). This included members of both ZANLA and ZIPRA. The unmitigated rivalry between the two groups continued to pose a serious threat to national unity and peace, however, especially in the Matabeleland and Midlands provinces.

When fierce fighting broke out between ZANLA and ZIPRA forces encamped at the Entumbane military cantonment in Bulawayo, the violence soon spread to other towns outside Harare, such as Chitungwiza. Ironically, the government deployed former Rhodesian Security Forces led by General Peter Walls to quell the fighting. It was reported that more than 300 people lost their lives, while scores – mostly former ZIPRA fighters – deserted from the army and took to the bush.

Amid these volatile circumstances, Prime Minister Mugabe committed his government to land reform. He created a new Ministry of Lands, Resettlement and Rural Development, and he announced that land reform would be necessary to alleviate over-population in the former Tribal Trust Lands and to expand the production potential of small-scale subsistence farmers. The stated goals of the ministry were to ensure that abandoned or underutilised land was being exploited to its fullest potential and providing oppor-tunities for unemployed, landless peasants.

Two decades later, the land issue would create a major crisis for Mugabe, his government and the country as a whole after frustrated peasants and ZANU-PF activists started to invade white-owned commercial farms.

3

Silencing divergent voices

*'Nothing in my life had prepared me for persecution at the
hands of a government led by black Africans.'*
— Joshua Mqabuko Nkomo, 1984

Gukurahundi

The first direct post-independence challenge to Mugabe's authority
came, rather expectedly, from his long-standing rival Joshua Nkomo,
the leader of ZAPU.

While Mugabe had displayed a discernible streak of intolerance
in Mozambique, his legendary narrow-mindedness was to cost
thousands of his compatriots their freedom and their lives in the
early years of Zimbabwe's independence. In what became known
as the Gukurahundi massacres, the ZNA carried out a ruthless
wave of violence, with most of the victims reported to be innocent
Ndebele civilians.

Beginning in early 1983, the horrific campaign was unleashed
by 5 Brigade, a unit of the ZNA that comprised former ZANLA
guerrillas exclusively. The brigade was trained by North Korean
military specialists in Nyanga for the purpose of quelling resistance to the fledgling Mugabe government in the Matabeleland
and Midlands provinces. The electorate in the regions concerned
had voted overwhelmingly against Mugabe's ZANU-PF party in

a massive display of support and loyalty to Nkomo's ZAPU in the 1980 elections. The resultant bad blood had been aggravated by virulent antagonism at the personal level between Nkomo and Mugabe's point man in the trouble-ridden Matabeleland, Enos Nkala, who was the most senior ZANU-PF functionary of Ndebele origin. Nkala was also extremely unpopular in this area.

The major difference between the two nationalist organisations was historical and, to a considerable extent, ethnic. During the war of liberation, ZANU drew the bulk of its supporters from among the Shona people of central, northern and eastern Zimbabwe, while enjoying strategic support from Beijing in the People's Republic of China. ZAPU, on the other hand, was backed by Moscow, and its members were largely Ndebele, the smaller of the country's two main ethnic groups.

In the Shona language, the word Gukurahundi has its origin in an idiom that, loosely translated, means 'the early rain that washes away the chaff from the previous harvest before the onset of the spring rains'. In the areas affected by the military campaign, Gukurahundi lasted from 1983 to late 1987.

In real terms, the onslaught on Matabeleland and parts of the Midlands was to silence any opposing political views emanating from supporters of Nkomo and ZAPU.

During the final stages of the Bush War, the two rival nationalist organisations, Mugabe's ZANU and Nkomo's ZAPU, had merged to present a united front against the Rhodesian government's predominantly white Security Forces. However, after the Lancaster House Agreement, Mugabe expressed a desire to campaign independently of Nkomo in the forthcoming general elections in February 1980. His strategy won the day, but Nkomo felt betrayed.

Following ZANU-PF's victory and Mugabe's becoming prime minister of independent Zimbabwe, disgruntled former guerrillas and supporters of ZAPU continued to pose a threat to the new government, culminating in the discovery of large caches of military hardware hidden on properties belonging to the party. This led to the emergence of South African–backed dissidents who launched a campaign to destabilise state and commercial farming infrastructure. There was a limited outbreak of violence carried out by ZIPRA malcontents against the civilian population in Matabeleland.

In early 1983, the Mugabe regime unleashed the red-bereted 5 Brigade in Matabeleland North Province in a crackdown ostensibly to counter this dissident activity. At the height of the brutal campaign, thousands of Ndebele people were summarily executed, tortured or captured by government forces. Estimates of victims of the Gukurahundi massacres range from 8 000 to 16 000, with some going up as high as 20 000. Ian Smith gave an estimate of more than 30 000 dead.

Such was the bloody price that the Ndebele people of southwestern Zimbabwe were forced to pay for their support, some of it legitimate, of a political organisation that opposed Mugabe at a time when he sought to establish a Marxist–Leninist one-party state. An end to the violence only came in December 1987, when Mugabe and Nkomo signed a Unity Accord, which heralded the advent of peace to Matabeleland.

The flight of Joshua Nkomo
Dr Joshua Nkomo, the leader of ZAPU, represented the ultimate political challenge to Robert Mugabe's intolerant leadership style.

While generally regarded as Ndebele, Nkomo was in fact a

member of the Kalanga tribe, a people descended from the Shona, who were conquered and assimilated by the Ndebele in the nineteenth century.

When he created his first cabinet, Mugabe refused to appoint Nkomo to the position of minister of defence, which the ZAPU leader had been expecting. But, after the intervention of Mugabe's wife, Sally, Nkomo was appointed as a minister without portfolio. He was, however, accused in 1982 of plotting a coup d'état against Mugabe. It was rumoured that South African double agents in Zimbabwe's Central Intelligence Organisation (CIO), attempting to cause disaffection between ZAPU and ZANU, planted arms on ZAPU-owned farms and then tipped off Mugabe about their existence. Given the gigantic quantity of weapons unearthed in the caches in question, the CIO double agents must have relied on external logistics to successfully and secretly transport the armaments.

In a public statement, Mugabe said, 'ZAPU and its leader, Dr Joshua Nkomo, are like a cobra in a house. The only way to deal effectively with a snake is to strike and destroy its head.'

Mugabe then unleashed 5 Brigade on Matabeleland in Operation Gukurahundi. Nkomo fled the country on 7 March 1983. The newly appointed minister of home affairs, Dr Herbert Sylvester Masiyiwa Ushewokunze, was widely reported in the newspapers as having claimed, to the amusement of his ZANU colleagues, that the ZAPU leader had illegally left the country while dressed as a woman.

Nkomo, however, firmly dismissed the rumour that he had escaped in any such disguise. 'I expected they would invent stupid stories about my flight,' he said. 'People will believe anything if they believe that.'

Then he added: 'Nothing in my life had prepared me for persecution at the hands of a government led by black Africans.'

In order to end the Gukurahundi massacres, Nkomo agreed in 1987 to the signing of the Unity Accord, by which he effectively consented to the swallowing of ZAPU by ZANU, thus creating a single party called ZANU-PF. With that, Mugabe's cherished dream of creating a one-party state in Zimbabwe became a reality. Some of Nkomo's more radical supporters accused their leader of selling out to their enemies – Mugabe and ZANU – and his influence started to diminish.

When asked many years later by Eliakim Sibanda, an assistant professor of history at the University of Winnipeg in Manitoba, Canada, why he signed the agreement with Mugabe, Nkomo was forthright in his response. He said that he had done it in order to stop the murder of the Ndebele people, who were the backbone of his party, and the killing of ZAPU politicians and organisers, who had been targeted by Zimbabwe's security forces since 1982. 'Mugabe and his Shona henchmen have always sought the extermination of the Ndebele,' Nkomo said.

In 1984, he recorded his many trials and tribulations at the hands of Mugabe in his own book, *The Story of My Life*. Nkomo, who was affectionately called Umdala Wethu ('our old man' in the Ndebele language) and Chibwechitedza (Shona for 'the slippery rock'), died a bitter and frustrated man on 1 July 1999.

Willowgate and other scandals
While the signing of the Unity Accord brought welcome peace and freedom to Matabeleland and the Midlands, those were not the only remarkable outcomes of the agreement between Mugabe and Nkomo.

After five years of operating under strict regulation, including the state of emergency and curfew imposed on the dissident-affected areas during Gukurahundi, the media, especially the press in Bulawayo, experienced a new sense of operational freedom. I was then editor of *The Chronicle*, the daily newspaper published by Zimbabwe Newspapers (1980) Ltd, a company in which government, through the Zimbabwe Mass Media Trust, was a majority share-holder to the tune of 51 per cent.

Whether by design or coincidence, as Gukurahundi paled into a painful memory, a new phenomenon crept onto centre stage – official corruption. As reports, rumours and allegations of corruption increased, President Mugabe took an unprecedented step. He demanded that Zimbabweans, and the media in particular, desist from making spurious allegations of corruption against members of his government. He said that those making such allegations should provide tangible evidence.

Vice President Simon Vengai Muzenda, newly appointed in 1988, endorsed these sentiments. The press was thus granted some leeway to investigate corruption, with the condition that only well-investigated allegations, supported by solid proof, were published.

Two cases of corruption had been uncovered at the time, these being the Paweni corruption scandal in Harare and the National Railways of Zimbabwe housing scandal in Bulawayo. During the Paweni trial in Harare, the name of social services minister Kumbirai Manyika Kangai had been mentioned as an accomplice in the scandal, which involved the inflation of transport charges for relief food supplies to rural areas following a drought in 1982. The Zimbabwe Newspapers flagship *The Herald* redacted the name of the minister from its coverage of this fascinating court case. Meanwhile,

The Chronicle, relying on coverage provided by ZIANA, the national news agency, revealed the name of Kangai as an alleged accomplice.

The impression was immediately created in the public's mind that *The Chronicle* in Bulawayo was more reliable than *The Herald* in Harare in the fight against corruption. Not surprisingly, when the sensational story broke about the corrupt acquisition of motor vehicles from Willowvale Mazda Motor Industries in Harare by top government ministers and the resale of the same vehicles at exorbitant markups, it was in *The Chronicle* that details of the massive corruption were investigated, documented and exposed.

Halfway through what became known as the Willowgate scandal saga, Mugabe summoned me to the State House in Harare and enjoined me not to publish any falsehoods about his ministers. We parted on a solemn undertaking by me that no falsehoods would be published about any government official, especially given that so many well-documented and incriminating truths were being uncovered daily about his ministers. When the full force of the implications of the scandal entered the public domain, Mugabe was forced to appoint Zimbabwe's first public inquiry, the Sandura Commission, headed by Judge President Wilson Runyararo Sandura and aided by attorneys Robert Atherstone Stumbles and Vernanda Cecily Ziyambi. The courtroom where the proceedings were conducted was packed to the rafters at every session, as ordinary citizens came to terms with the unprecedented spectacle of usually haughty politicians being humbled or humiliated.

The *Washington Post* reported in the US in April 1989 that the commission's hearings had 'struck a deep chord' in Zimbabwe, where citizens had come to resent the perceived growing corruption of government officials. Michael Hiltzik of the *Los Angeles*

Times reported: 'What followed was a public inquiry into official corruption that has no parallel in sub-Saharan Africa and little enough anywhere else in the world. In countries from Kenya to Zaire, such corruption is institutionalized, explained away or kept safely out of the media.'

But, back in Zimbabwe, Mugabe was far from amused by the unfolding events, which culminated in Maurice Tapfumaneyi Nyagumbo, one of the ministers incriminated in multiple cases of corruption, committing suicide. A top ally of Mugabe, Nyagumbo had been instrumental in the illegal purchase and money-spinning disposal of thirty-six vehicles.

Before the first hearing of the Sandura Commission was held in Harare, Zimbabwe Newspapers dismissed my deputy editor, Davison Smiler Maruziva, and me from our positions at *The Chronicle* in Bulawayo.

Mugabe, who not so long before had granted authority for well-documented cases of corruption to be published, did a sudden about-turn. He accused me of being overzealous in that I had allegedly labelled his ministers as being corrupt. He said that I could not rightfully complain, as I had been promoted to head office on a higher salary. It was of no consequence to His Excellency that the position concerned had been specially created to get me away from editorial work.

As if that were not clear enough evidence of Mugabe's intolerance, Frederick Makamure Masiiwa Shava, the one Willowgate minister who had a taste of the inside of prison after he lied to the Sandura Commission and was convicted of perjury, was spirited out after only one night of incarceration. A hastily convened Politburo meeting took the decision to exonerate Shava.

'Who among us has *not* lied?' the president is quoted in *The Chronicle* as asking the assembled ZANU-PF leaders with what sounded like profound logic. 'Yesterday, you were with your girl-friend and told your wife that you were with the President.'

On that illogical note, after months of hard work by *The Chronicle* and the Sandura Commission, the Willowgate scandal fizzled into nothing. In the fullness of time, Shava was rescued from ignominy and appointed first as Zimbabwe's ambassador to China and then as the country's representative at the United Nations Mission in New York.

Edgar Tekere, the thorn in Mugabe's side

In his heyday as ZANU-PF secretary-general, Edgar Tekere, popularly known by his nickname Two Boy, was one of Mugabe's political allies. The two had travelled together on that epoch-making journey to Mozambique back in 1975, accompanied by Chief Rekayi Tangwena.

Tekere, who was a founding member and the second and last secretary-general of ZANU, was responsible for organising the party during the Lancaster House talks, and he briefly served as a cabinet minister. He was dropped from this position, however, after appearing in a sensational court case to face the accusation of murdering a white commercial farmer.

After Tekere criticised corruption in ZANU-PF in August 1984, he was carried shoulder-high from the party's congress. Predictably, Tekere's growing popularity as a potential rival did not sit well with Mugabe. It led to estrangement between the two once-close cronies. Tekere was increasingly seen as the leader of a rival faction to Mugabe within ZANU-PF, and he was dismissed as secretary-general (Mugabe then took over that post as well and held it for the rest of his time in power).

Buoyed by the Willowgate scandal in October 1988 and supported by University of Zimbabwe students under the leadership of the charismatic Arthur Guseni Oliver Mutambara, Tekere intensified his consistent criticism of corruption. As a result, he was expelled from ZANU-PF. Tekere had also vehemently opposed Mugabe's one-party-state mantra.

Forming his own political party, the Zimbabwe Unity Movement (ZUM), Tekere challenged Mugabe in the 1990 presidential elections. While Tekere garnered 413 840 votes, Mugabe swept the polls with 2 026 976, amid charges of massive election-rigging by ZANU-PF. It was common knowledge that ZANU-PF activists had subjected ZUM supporters to widespread attacks of violence, with five of the party's candidates being murdered.

Tekere's autobiography, *A Lifetime of Struggle*, was published in 2007. He devoted a substantial portion of it to his none-too-complimentary views on Mugabe and ZANU-PF. But Mugabe dismissed Tekere's book as the work of an unbalanced mind, while dismissing the author from ZANU-PF for the second time.

Nevertheless, as if to spite their 'Dear Leader', the ZANU-PF Politburo unanimously declared Tekere a national hero as a prelude to his interment at the National Heroes' Acre in Harare in June 2011. Mugabe's abhorrence and intolerance of Tekere could not reverse this decision.

The intrepid Dzikamai Mavhaire

Masvingo politician Dzikamai Mavhaire was a relatively obscure legislator until he hit a political jackpot in 1997.

The major turnaround in his fortunes occurred when he summoned sufficient mettle to voice a statement so obvious that nearly every politician in the House of Assembly had been dying to articulate it but were too petrified to do so.

Standing up in the House, Mavhaire openly called on President Mugabe, who was then seventy-three years old, to resign from office. So incensed were his Mugabe-fearing fellow members of Parliament that Mavhaire found himself out on the street in no time. He was expelled from ZANU-PF.

Media reports later suggested, rather uncharitably, that Mavhaire's statement had instantly transformed him from a long-term legislator into a fruit vendor, selling oranges from the back of a ramshackle vehicle.

'As soon as I uttered those words there was total silence in a Parliament which was dominated and controlled by ruling party MPs,' Mavhaire was quoted as saying in *The Zimbabwean*, a UK-based newspaper.

Unsurprisingly, the common sense in Mavhaire's comment was soundly ignored. The president's grip on his supporters – and on those who opposed him – was simply too strong.

The challenge of the MDC

The Movement for Democratic Change (MDC), a political party established under the leadership of trade unionist Morgan Richard Tsvangirai in September 1999, became the most viable opposition organisation launched in independent Zimbabwe. The new political party emerged from the ranks of the Zimbabwe Congress of Trade Unions (ZCTU). It incorporated the National Constitutional Assembly (NCA), led by Professor Lovemore Madhuku;

the national student movement; and various militant civil society organisations.

The party spearheaded a successful campaign to reject a proposed new constitution when it galvanised its broad coalition of constituent members in a referendum held in February 2000. Building on the success of its crusade for a 'No' vote, the MDC campaigned for parliamentary elections held in June 2000, in which, according to Jonathan Moyo, 'the opposition shocked the ruling party into serious self-doubt by getting 57 out of 120 seats'.

The MDC, therefore, developed into the official opposition party and became the most serious challenge to President Mugabe and the ruling ZANU-PF within a year of its launch.

ZANU-PF's reaction to this new threat was typical of the party's infamous intolerance of political opposition. Like the UANC of Abel Muzorewa soon after independence, as well as Joshua Nkomo's PF-ZAPU, Ndabaningi Sithole's ZANU-Ndonga and the ZUM of Edgar Tekere, Tsvangirai's party was subjected to orgies of savage violence. (Tsvangirai's party adopted the name MDC-T after a breakaway faction retained the original MDC handle in 2005.)

Tekere had stood against Mugabe for the first time in 1990. Supporters of the ZUM became targets of extensive political violence. In the 1996 elections, Mugabe was challenged by Muzorewa and Sithole, both of whom later withdrew their candidature when violence was unleashed against UANC and ZANU-Ndonga supporters in circumstances where the electoral field favoured the ruling ZANU-PF. Mugabe secured a runaway victory, with 90 per cent of the votes.

The tables were turned against Mugabe, however, in the following presidential elections of 2002, which were the first since the formation of the MDC in 1999. Although Mugabe secured yet another victory, his margin was significantly reduced from the 92.76 per cent of 1996 to only 56.2 per cent against the newcomer Morgan Tsvangirai, who garnered an impressive 42 per cent in his first showing and in circumstances of widespread violence against opposition supporters.

Over the next few years, the violence against the MDC-T continued to escalate. On 11 March 2007, heavily armed riot police were deployed to prevent an MDC-T prayer meeting dubbed 'Save Zimbabwe' from taking place. They used tear gas and water cannons to disband this demonstration against the government. The protesters responded by setting up barricades of combustible materials across streets in the suburb of Highfield and pelting the police with stones, resulting in skirmishes breaking out.

Andrew Meldrum, a correspondent for *The Guardian* in London, reported from Johannesburg that Morgan Tsvangirai had sustained severe head injuries and that the police had shot one protester, Gift Tandare, dead. The police then arrested Tsvangirai, along with 110 of his supporters. Tsvangirai was reported to have been bleeding heavily while he was kept in a holding cell that night. He was nevertheless denied access to lawyers or to medical attention, resulting in the Zimbabwe Lawyers for Human Rights intervening. They applied for an urgent court order for them to secure access to Tsvangirai and for the MDC-T leader to be attended to by doctors.

Meldrum, who had reported from Harare for twenty-three years since Zimbabwe's independence, had himself been expelled from the country in 2003 because of his constant exposure of ZANU-PF's violence against their political opposition. Two years earlier, in 2001, both the BBC and CNN had been similarly banned from covering Zimbabwe; in the case of the BBC, it was for 'reporting lies about the land seizures'. Jonathan Moyo, then minister of information, announced that he was 'suspending all accreditation of BBC correspondents in Zimbabwe'.

There was also violence after the general elections of 29 March 2008, which many people believed were won by Tsvangirai's MDC. The results were not released for over a month, and when they were, it transpired that Tsvangirai had won 47.9 per cent of the vote compared to Mugabe's 43.2 per cent. Because neither candidate had won an outright majority, a run-off election was held on 27 June. But Tsvangirai withdrew from the run-off, citing an escalation in state-sponsored violence against his supporters.

Tsvangirai claimed that eighty-five members of the MDC-T had been killed during the three-month period between the two rounds of voting on 29 March and 27 June 2008. He said that 10 000 MDC-T supporters had been injured, while 200 000 had been rendered homeless by ZANU-PF militias, state security agents and the ubiquitous war veterans.

Mugabe won the second round with a massive majority of 85.5 per cent against Tsvangirai, whose name had remained on the ballot paper after his withdrawal.

ZANU-PF generally regarded the MDC-T as a mouthpiece for white commercial farmers, many of whom had openly pledged financial support for the new party. The invasion of white-owned commercial farms thus targeted the apparent backbone of the MDC-T's support.

One of the most horrific acts of political violence perpetrated by ZANU-PF against the opposition was the brutal murder of MDC-T activists Tichaona Chiminya and Talent Mabika during the farm invasions in 2000. The two of them were gunned down with AK-47 rifles in broad daylight in the Buhera District of Manicaland Province before their vehicle was petrol-bombed and set ablaze. Joseph Mwale, a CIO operative, and his fellow accomplice, war veteran Kainos 'Kitsiyatota' Zimunya, were identified as the perpetrators of this reprehensible act. They were never arrested or prosecuted.

The arrests of Mark Chavunduka and Ray Choto

Mark Gova Chavunduka was one of the luminaries of Zimbabwe's turbulent journalism profession. He became the editor of the best-selling *Parade* magazine in 1991, at the age of twenty-four, and then of *The Standard* newspaper in 1997.

In 1999, one of *The Standard's* writers, Ray Choto, reported on a mutiny by Zimbabwean soldiers over the deployment of troops to the DRC. The state's response to the journalist and his editor was brutal. According to the British *Guardian*,

> For more than 10 days, Chavunduka and Choto were detained incommunicado at Cranborne Barracks [in] Harare. Their lawyer, Simon Bull, said both men were subjected to electric shocks on their genitals, hands and feet by military interrogators, and had their heads submerged in drums of water. They were also blindfolded, stripped naked, made to do push-ups in the rain, and to roll in wet grass to clean the blood from their bodies after beating.
>
> Independent medical sources confirmed the torture allegations, and the incident, seen by many as the most outrageous

attack on press freedom in Zimbabwe since independence, drew worldwide condemnation.

President Mugabe, however, refused to condemn the torture. Instead, he threatened 'very stern measures' against the independent press, warned writers not to antagonize the army, and ignored a court order to release the two journalists.

Choto was released after three days in military custody, and Chavunduka after ten days.

Chavunduka died in 2002 of an unspecified illness at the age of thirty-six. An obituary was published in the *Guardian*:

> As founding editor of Zimbabwe's independent Sunday newspaper, *The Standard*, the award-winning journalist and publisher, Mark Chavunduka ... was a champion for media freedom in southern Africa.
>
> His paper became a symbol of resistance among his country's journalists, and a thorn in the flesh of President Robert Mugabe's government. He exposed the corruption and political intimidation rife in Zimbabwe, and his outspokenness made *The Standard* an internationally recognized voice for those opposed to Mugabe's tyranny.

After his release from prison in 1999, Chavunduka was treated for post-traumatic stress disorder at the Medical Foundation for the Treatment of Torture Victims in London. After going to Harvard as a Nieman Fellow, he returned to Zimbabwe. 'My family all said I should have stayed in the US,' he said, 'but I am so angry about the way we were treated, and I won't give the government the satisfaction of knowing I've run away.'

The treatment of journalists such as Chavunduka and Choto underscores the lengths to which the Mugabe regime went in its bid to silence competing voices.

The *Daily News* saga

The *Daily News*, a privately owned newspaper, was founded under my editorship in 1999. Published with the motto 'Telling it like it is', in a Zimbabwe where the government preferred for much that happened to be swept under the carpet as a matter of routine, disregarding public interest, the newspaper was bound to incur the authorities' wrath. Most incensed were President Mugabe himself and Jonathan Moyo, the notorious information and broadcasting minister.

While the *Daily News* rapidly became Zimbabwe's best-selling newspaper, it was characterised by both Mugabe and Moyo as a mouthpiece of the opposition party, the MDC; as a puppet of Western imperialist interests; and as an impudent supporter of the commercial farming sector during the widely condemned lawlessness of the 2000 farm invasions. In the highly charged and polarised political environment, retribution was not too long in coming. The newspaper's courageous journalists became targets of spurious arrests, intimidation and threats from powerful politicians, and of violence by members of the security forces, the war veteran community and ZANU-PF activists. I was arrested on six different occasions, on baseless charges. An agent, Bernard Masara, was hired and paid by Innocent Mugabe – one of Mugabe's nephews and a top CIO official – to assassinate me. A last-minute change of heart on Masara's part saved my life.

The newspaper suffered two bombings allegedly by the Zimbabwean security forces. The first was a hand-grenade attack on the building housing the newspaper's offices along Samora Machel Avenue, while, in the second attack, the *Daily News*'s printing press was totally destroyed.

In 1998, the Mugabe administration deployed elements of the ZNA to the Democratic Republic of Congo (DRC). This decision was taken arbitrarily by Mugabe himself, without consulting either Parliament or his cabinet. He was, perhaps, the most ardent supporter of intervention on behalf of the beleaguered DRC president Laurent-Désiré Kabila. On 16 January 2001, Kabila was shot and wounded at the presidential palace in Kinshasa. The government announced that Kabila was still alive when he was flown to Zimbabwe for intensive-care treatment. Two days later, it was announced that Kabila had died from his injuries. His remains were returned for a state funeral on 26 January.

The *Daily News* reported that there was jubilation in the streets of Harare at the news of Kabila's death. The following day, 27 January, Jonathan Moyo appeared on prime-time television. He said that the *Daily News* had gone too far and needed to be silenced. In the middle of the night on 28 January 2001, the newspaper's printing press was destroyed by a bomb placed inside its factory in the Lochinvar industrial area.

In October 2017, I unearthed details of how the plot to bomb the printing press was allegedly hatched at the home of former ZDF commander General Solomon Tapfumaneyi Mujuru and then passed over to Menard Livingstone Muzariri, deputy director general of the CIO, for planning. Once the details were established, the army was brought back in for a joint execution.

In the end, the Mugabe government banned the *Daily News* and the *Daily News on Sunday*, as well as another privately owned weekly newspaper, *The Tribune*, in September 2003.

Operation Murambatsvina

Operation Murambatsvina, also officially known as Operation Restore Order, was a campaign launched in 2005 to silence an urban population that had drifted into the MDC camp under opposition leader Morgan Tsvangirai.

The timing of the massive clean-up operation, so soon after the disputed parliamentary elections held on 31 March 2005, in which ZANU-PF had not fared as well as had been expected, prompted commentators to state that there were ulterior motives for the demolition of supposedly illegal urban residential and commercial structures. The obvious motive was a bid to weaken the political opposition in its urban strongholds.

Affected citizens characterised the operation as 'Zimbabwe's tsunami'. The crackdown affected most of the country's major cities, with the government stating that it intended to widen the operation to include rural farming areas.

The United Nations has estimated that Murambatsvina led to a loss of employment for 700 000 people, while affecting a further 2.4 million people countrywide. Earlier, the Zimbabwe Human Rights NGO Forum estimated that 64 677 families had been displaced, representing a total of approximately 323 385 people.

Those affected by the widely condemned clearances were all left in need of emergency relief and resettlement following the loss of their homes and livelihoods. A report published in 2005 by Dr Anna Tibaijuka, the executive director of the United Nations Human Settlements Programme, described the operation as a disastrous venture that had violated international law and led to a serious humanitarian crisis. Tibaijuka's report called for all demolitions to be stopped immediately. The ruling ZANU-PF party was blamed for the government's actions, which were described as being indiscriminate, unjustified and conducted without regard for human suffering.

Professor Jameson Kurasha, one of President Mugabe's nephews and the chairperson of a commission established to oversee the affairs of the city of Harare, initiated Operation Murambatsvina weeks after the disputed 2005 elections were held. The nine-member Kurasha Commission was appointed directly by Dr Ignatius Morgan Chiminya Chombo, the minister of local government and urban and rural development. *The Standard* commented that 'President Mugabe, through the Minister of Local Government, Urban and Rural Development, Ignatius Chombo, is now effectively in control of the City of Harare'.

While Mugabe suggested that the clearances were necessary to carry out a clean-up campaign, it was clear that the operation was politically motivated, with an agenda to ensure the political survival of a ZANU-PF seriously threatened by its opposition, the MDC.

'It is these people who have been making the country ungovernable by their criminal activities actually,' the police commissioner Augustine Chihuri commented, saying that Operation Murambatsvina was meant to 'clean the country of the crawling mass of maggots bent on destroying the economy'.

The police were in the forefront of demolishing residential and commercial structures. They had the support of the army and the National Youth Service, who sometimes enforced the evictions at gunpoint. Victims were ordered to leave urban areas – the strongholds of the opposition – and to return to rural areas, where ZANU-PF was more assured of support. Otherwise, they faced further abuse from their tormentors. 'There is nobody in Zimbabwe who does not have a rural home,' education minister Aeneas Soko Chigwedere pointed out rather sardonically.

The MDC has argued, perhaps with ample justification, that the Mugabe government's prime motivation in unleashing Murambatsvina on the urban poor was to discipline them for voting for the opposition during the March parliamentary elections. The cities are traditionally MDC strongholds, and the ad hoc Harare Commission that initiated the operation was in fact only established by the minister of local government as a stopgap measure to countermand the governing powers of the elected MDC City Council, regardless of whether some of the victims of Murambatsvina were ZANU-PF supporters or war veterans.

This effort by Operation Murambatsvina in 2005 to weaken the political opposition of the day echoed the Gukurahundi campaign in the early 1980s. And both were launched with connotations of being massive clean-ups.

Operation Murambatsvina targeted the MDC of Morgan Tsvangirai, a fellow Shona clansman of Mugabe, while Gukurahundi had focused on ZAPU supporters and their leader, Joshua Nkomo, an Ndebele/Kalanga politician. Meanwhile, the land invasions that started in 2002 targeted white commercial farmers. It appears that Mugabe's quest for political self-preservation had little regard for race or ethnicity. In retrospect, his actions make clear his broad intolerance of divergent views and of anyone regarded as supporting the 'wrong' party.

Over the decades since independence, Mugabe managed to keep the challenges posed against his party and himself under control, often by resorting to the expedient use of violence. Joshua Nkomo, Abel Muzorewa, Ndabaningi Sithole, Edgar Tekere and Morgan Tsvangirai were among the many he successfully subdued, and they would not be the last.

4

From breadbasket to basket case

'You have inherited a jewel in Africa. Don't tarnish it.'
– President Julius Nyerere to Prime Minister Mugabe, 1980

It took President Mugabe just over two decades to bring a Zimbabwe that possessed much promise of peace and prosperity down to its knees. By then, to the chagrin of increasingly disillusioned Zimbabweans, he had effectively tarnished this African jewel, as the country had been described by Julius Nyerere, the president of Tanzania.

Nyerere's comment was likely inspired by the magnificence of the Zimbabwean capital that he encountered while on a state visit in December 1980. Visiting from the poverty-stricken conditions that were common at the time in his own capital city, Dar es Salaam, it was hardly surprising that Nyerere would equate Harare to a shining jewel.

Tanzania had been experiencing serious economic hardships, compounded by a serious shortage of many basic commodities and a dilapidated infrastructure. Despite the fact that the Rhodesia of Smith's regime had been buffeted by fifteen years of international sanctions, Mugabe still inherited a sound economy and, by the time of Nyerere's visit, Zimbabweans had not yet been subjected to the level of parlous economic hardships that were commonplace in Tanzania, Zambia, Malawi and Mozambique. These countries had gained independence much earlier than Zimbabwe had in 1980. Tanzania became independent in 1963, Zambia and Malawi achieved full independence status in 1964, and Mozambique followed in 1975.

When Mugabe came to power, he took over a country with a booming agricultural sector, which produced tobacco, maize and horticultural products for export. The tobacco industry in particular was thriving. The production of wheat was much higher than in the past, and in the early years of independence, Zimbabwe became the breadbasket of southern Africa. Another driver of the Zimbabwean economy was the well-established mining sector, which profited from an abundance of natural resources, such as chrome, coal, copper, gold, nickel and iron ore. In fact, the early development of Rhodesia had been spurred on by the discovery of gold by European settlers.

Zimbabwe's economy also benefited from possessing a wealth of skilled human resources, which allowed for a well-developed industrial sector, as well as well-maintained road and railway networks. More significantly, at independence, Zimbabwe's currency was robust; it was similar in strength to both the British pound sterling and the US dollar at their official exchange rates.

While economic indicators for Zimbabwe were therefore strong, Mugabe nevertheless managed, over the course of his rule, to squander this priceless inheritance and ruin any existing goodwill. He achieved this through a combination of mismanagement of the economy, ill-advised economic policies, and a failure to rein in epidemic corruption. By 2010, Zimbabwe's status as the breadbasket of the region had degenerated to that of being a basket case: one of

Africa's most productive economies had become a shambles. The population of a country with a farming sector that was once an exporter of beef and maize had now become desperate for food. Many Zimbabweans had to depend on humanitarian food hand-outs, such as maize donated by Australia through the United Nations World Food Programme.

A number of decisions by Mugabe and policies made by his government contributed to this decline. From 1990 to 1996, Mugabe's government embarked on an Economic Structural Adjustment Programme (ESAP), which had serious negative effects on Zimbabwe's economy. Massive inflation and unemployment figures that exceeded more than 90 per cent began to characterise its performance, as once-productive factories either scaled down operations or closed altogether.

In an article for the *Southern Africa Report* in 1996, Richard Saunders, the report's Zimbabwe correspondent, says that Zimbabwe's ESAP was meant to

herald a new era of modernised, competitive, export-led indus-trialisation.

But, despite a high-performing economy in its first decade of independence, the country now appears firmly lodged in a quagmire of mounting debt and erratic growth in the wake of five years of ESAP-mandated reforms.

In a short time, ESAP's World Bank-inspired reforms [have] ripped into the existing economic and social infrastruc-ture, shifting the focus of many mass-oriented development social programs away from redistribution towards manage-ment of defined and limited, even declining, public resources.

Soon after independence, the Mugabe government had introduced populist policies, such as the provision of free education and health services, with a promise to provide housing for all by the year 2000. To support the cost of such schemes, the administration overspent without restraint – a damaging practice that continued throughout the long period of Mugabe's reign. This provision of unrealistic social services was short-lived. They were soon replaced by shortages of medical services and drugs in the health sector and ramshackle schools that were lacking in teachers, books and equipment. The lack of accommodation in the urban areas spiralled, causing the emergence of sprawling shanty settlements. The absence of basic services such as running water and sewerage systems became a feature of haphazard urban development and a headache for town planners. The government responded by unleashing Operation Murambatsvina in 2005, ostensibly in a bid to demolish the illegal settlements and combat infectious diseases. Over the course of the campaign, hundreds of thousands of people lost their homes and livelihoods, and over two million suffered from the indirect consequences of the brutal crackdown.

Within one generation, Mugabe had systematically – and with breathtaking precision – turned Zimbabwe upside down.

Compensation to war veterans

The veterans of Zimbabwe's war of liberation, whose numbers had mushroomed to 50 000 strong by 1997, had felt increasingly neglected over the years since independence. The fortunes of the ZANU-PF leadership had been changing for the better, with new lifestyles steeped in luxury, while the war veterans, their former allies who had borne the brunt of the liberation struggle, still wallowed in poverty.

In 1997, the veterans embarked on a series of protests against Mugabe, who succumbed to the mounting pressure from this increasingly powerful wing of his party. The government awarded each veteran a lump sum of Z$50 000 in gratuities plus monthly pensions of Z$2 000, none of which was budgeted for by the Treasury. As a result, the Zimbabwe economy responded negatively. In fact, these unplanned payments are widely viewed as having heralded Zimbabwe's economic collapse.

On 14 November 1997, exactly twenty years before Mugabe was finally overthrown from power in 2017, Zimbabwean dollar lost its value against the US dollar by a whopping 71.5 per cent. The day is remembered as 'Black Friday'.

Arbitrary deployment of the military to the DRC

In 1998, Zimbabweans were up in arms when the Mugabe administration deployed ZNA troops to the DRC without consulting either Parliament or the cabinet, and without informing the population at large. About 11 000 Zimbabwean troops were fighting at the time alongside President Laurent Kabila's forces in the DRC against rebels backed by Rwanda and Uganda.

As the war in the DRC continued, the Air Force of Zimbabwe was reported to have made particularly effective use of its air power by making repeated strikes with its fighter jets. As losses of hardware burgeoned, Western donors, mostly the International Monetary Fund and the World Bank, decided to deny the Mugabe government the astounding figure of US$600 million in foreign currency that was required for the purchase of spare parts for the vehicles then deployed in the war zone.

The DRC intervention was a costly exercise both financially and politically, with many votes lost to the emergent MDC opposition party, which, within a year of its formation in September 1999, made an impressive showing in the June 2000 elections.

Speaking two months later, in August 2000, finance minister Simba Herbert Stanley Makoni was quoted by the BBC as having told Parliament that Zimbabwe could not sustain the cost of its military intervention in the DRC for much longer. The country had apparently spent US$200 million over a period of two years since its involvement in the foreign war. Some experts dismissed Makoni's figure as too conservative, with one report quoting military officials as privately estimating the cost of the foreign intervention at US$15 million a month.

On 19 October 1998, the Zimbabwe Human Rights NGO Forum issued a press release that aptly captured the prevailing sentiment among concerned Zimbabweans. 'Without a mandate from Parliament,' the statement read, 'Zimbabwean troops are now being deployed in the eastern portion of the DRC which could result in a greater number of casualties and enormous financial cost. We are concerned about the lack of transparency in disclosing the exact number of Zimbabwean casualties.'

Fast-track land programme

While Zimbabwe was confronted by a vast array of economic woes, the one that broke the camel's back was the controversial fast-track land programme, which became a turning point in President Mugabe's succession of catastrophic blunders. In the year 2000, he orchestrated violent invasions of white-owned commercial farmlands, without government making adequate preparations for the exercise.

While a redress of the racist land-distribution policies of previous colonial administrations had been a battle cry of the nationalist struggle for liberation, the violent and haphazard land-redistribution programme implemented by the Mugabe government became a matter of grievous concern, especially among Zimbabwe's Western donor supporters.

The commercial farms, which were targeted mostly by liberation-war veterans, ZANU-PF activists, and government ministers and officials, were then the foundation of Zimbabwe's flourishing agricultural sector. Most of the new owners failed to work the land productively.

During the Lancaster House Conference, the issue of land reform had emerged as being critical. Both Mugabe and the ZAPU leader, Joshua Nkomo, had insisted on the redistribution of land – by compulsory seizure, without compensation – as a precondition to a negotiated peace settlement. This demand reflected the prevailing sentiment among the guerrilla fighters that a free allocation of land would be their legitimate entitlement in return for their sacrifice in fighting to dislodge Ian Smith's white minority Rhodesian Front regime. This expectation was also strong among the rural population, who had hosted and supported the guerrillas during the Bush War.

But the British government, which mediated the talks, proposed a constitutional clause to guarantee property ownership as an inalienable constitutional right. The British were anxious to prevent a mass exodus of white farmers, which might precipitate an economic collapse of the newly independent country. The clause, enshrined in Section 16 of the Zimbabwean Constitution of 1980, was thus viewed by some observers as a 'kith and kin' clause to protect the interests of the minority white population.

But Lord Carrington, who chaired the Lancaster House Conference, was equally anxious to secure the support of the externally based Zimbabwean nationalist leaders. To this end, he announced it as a condition that the UK would assist the proposed land-resettlement programme with technical assistance and financial aid.

The newly established Ministry of Lands, Resettlement and Redevelopment of Zimbabwe lacked both the necessary initiative and the trained personnel required to properly plan and implement the envisaged wide-scale resettlement programme. Progress was slow as a result. But in 1986, the Mugabe government cited financial constraints and an ongoing drought as the two overriding factors influencing the slow progress of land reform and redistribution.

A year before, Parliament had passed the Land Acquisition Act, which empowered the government to claim commercial farmland adjacent to the former Tribal Trust Lands and to mark tracts of that land for resettlement purposes, if the white owners were willing to sell. The Act, therefore, gave the Mugabe government first right to purchase excess land for redistribution to the poor and landless.

The vocal former guerrillas of the Zimbabwe National Liberation War Veterans Association (ZNLWVA) began to make radical demands for an immediate redistribution of land in their favour. They adopted the position that all land in white hands in Zimbabwe should rightfully be transferred to them, in keeping with promises made to ZANLA and ZIPRA fighters as they had waged the war of liberation. Their demand was viewed as quite legitimate, given the injustice and blatant racial discrimination of land appropriation by the white settlers at the time of the country's colonisation in 1890. This position was reinforced by demands for accelerated land reform, which emanated from urban blacks, who were more affluent than their rural counterparts and were therefore likely motivated by a wish to exploit the prospects of profitable commercial farming, especially if they were to receive public assistance.

The white population of Zimbabwe, constituting a mere 2 per cent or less of the total population, owned 70 per cent of the land. For seventeen years after independence, the government had prevaricated on the sensitive land-redistribution issue, while making promises about land reform that remained largely unfulfilled. Then, in 1997, while reeling from the disastrous effects of an economic meltdown, the embattled Mugabe suddenly published a list of 1 503 commercial farms, totalling over five million hectares, for takeover. He said that these farms had been earmarked for seizure without compensation being paid to their owners. They comprised half of the country's commercial farms.

'The demand and need for land by our people is now overwhelming,' Mugabe announced. 'If the British government wants us to compensate its children it must give us the money, or it does the compensation itself.'

Even the rural population had become restless at the slow pace of the government's land-resettlement process. As a result, a total of 300 villagers from twenty villages in the Svosve communal area near the town of Marondera moved onto three adjacent white-owned commercial farms. This move in Mashonaland East Province in June and July 1998 signalled the first significant step in the drawn-out revolution to dispossess the white commercial farming community of their land.

The militant war veterans' association organised people, mostly their members and other ZANU-PF activists, to invade white-owned commercial farms and forcibly remove their owners and workers. Many of the latter were immigrants, mostly from Malawi,

Zambia and Mozambique. Violence was common in these evictions, and the targeted farmers and workers often departed traumatised and with no possessions. Seven farmers and a large number of farm workers and family members were reported to have been killed during the farm invasions.

At the onset of the farm invasions, land totalling 110 000 square kilometres was seized by the invaders. The workers, most of whom considered the farms as their only home, were excluded from the resettlements. And because a large number were of foreign origin, they did not have a local rural home to return to.

The ensuing international outcry was predictable, and the economy plummeted further. The white farmers claimed that the proposed expropriation of land was merely a ploy to facilitate the theft of the country's best land by cabinet ministers and other powerful individuals aligned with ZANU-PF who wanted to turn the farmhouses – some of them exquisitely built – into retirement villas. There was an element of truth in this assertion. No serious farming activity took place on many of the seized farms.

Some of the new farmers, many chosen on the basis of their links to ZANU-PF, either did not possess any discernible commitment to meaningful farming or lacked experience with modern agricultural practices. They didn't have access to financial assistance to fund any commercial farming activity, and the situation was aggravated by the fact that the new settlers had no title deeds to offer financial institutions as collateral when applying for loans. A weakness of the fast-track land programme was that the government had not planned for the settlers' empowerment by imparting the necessary farming skills. In short, the programme was bereft of the technical assistance and financial-aid elements envisaged two decades earlier at the Lancaster House Conference. Many of the productive farms were soon abandoned, and the farmhouses were extensively vandalised. On cattle ranches, breeding stock was slaughtered for food or sold off.

'Time is short, and the government doesn't have focus,' David Hasluck, the executive director of the largely white Commercial Farmers' Union said in an interview for the *New York Times*. He was speaking in frustration when not a single farm had been bought, or even assessed, after some 200 farms had been made available for sale and approximately US$800 million in grants and loans from donors and banks had been offered. This violated the condition that the land would be paid for and that it would be allocated to poor or landless people who would be properly settled, instead of just being dumped.

In due course, Zimbabwe's commercial farming sector, which provided the country's primary source of foreign currency earnings, collapsed, which aggravated the ruin of the economy. Naturally, it was not white skin that was crucial to the success of the Rhodesian commercial farming sector. Rather, it was the availability of farming skills, inputs and financial resources, as later provided by the Mugabe government's Command Agriculture Programme, which helped to make commercial farming an economic success. Unfortunately, this came nearly two decades after the onset of the violence and controversy that surrounded Zimbabwe's land-redistribution programme in 2000.

Zimbabwe's hyperinflation
Zimbabwe's runaway hyperinflation can be traced back to the late 1990s, towards the end of the country's costly military involvement

in the DRC. Since then, the performance of the Zimbabwean economy has been afflicted by a long period of currency instability.

When Simba Makoni was brought into government as finance minister in June 2000, he was charged with the task of reversing the country's severe economic decline. But one of his tactical mistakes was to incur the wrath of the president by supporting proposals for the devaluation of the Zimbabwean dollar, a policy that Mugabe vehemently opposed.

Zimbabwe's economy was in even greater doldrums when Makoni was replaced in August 2002 with Herbert Murerwa, who had been Zimbabwe's ambassador to the UK. Manufacturing output continued to suffer, and by 2005 it had fallen by 29 per cent. Over the next two years, it dropped by a further 26 and 28 per cent, while unemployment escalated to a shocking 80 per cent.

By mid-November 2008, Zimbabwe's inflation was estimated at 79.6 billion per cent, the highest level of inflation ever reached by any country in the world. This statistic exceeded even inflation rates of nations at war.

Typically, the Mugabe government blamed the hyperinflation on the ongoing economic sanctions imposed on Zimbabwe by the International Monetary Fund, the European Union and the US. Strictly speaking, the sanctions were aimed specifically at the government of Zimbabwe. They also entailed asset freezes and visa denials that targeted 200 specific individuals who were closely linked to Mugabe and his administration.

The Reserve Bank of Zimbabwe under mercurial governor Gideon Gorno was reported to have started producing banknotes faster in order to satisfy the unfulfilled demands of the war veterans – who were seen as a crucial pillar of Mugabe's support – and to offset the higher prices caused by the serious dislocation of organised agriculture. The spiral of inflation quickly spun out of control. In January 2009, state media reported that the Reserve Bank of Zimbabwe was due to introduce an astronomical $100-trillion banknote, worth only about US$33 on the black market, in a bid to alleviate serious cash shortages.

After the establishment of the Government of National Unity (GNU) in 2009, Zimbabwe stopped printing its own currency. The Reserve Bank introduced the adoption and use of currencies from other countries, including South Africa, Great Britain, China and the United States. It was the US dollar that unofficially acquired the status of the official currency of Zimbabwe. In June 2015, the central bank announced plans to completely switch over to the US dollar as the official currency of Zimbabwe by the end of the year.

Just how Mugabe managed to reduce so prosperous a nation, which was endowed with so many natural and human resources, to such levels of destitution during his presidency makes for a benchmark study in misgovernance.

5

From 'small house'
to First Lady

'South African President Jacob Zuma has many wives. I admire
him because he stands for what he wants.'
                    — First Lady Grace Mugabe, 2014

My first real exposure to Grace Mugabe was through an interview
with her on the South African television station SABC 3 that aired
on 2 June 2013. It was conducted by South African journalist Dali
Tambo and was generously titled 'Grace Mugabe Reveals All'.

The interviews, held in the Mugabes' home, was a public relations exercise of extraordinary proportions for the family. Grace
Mugabe, the First Lady, was accorded a matchless opportunity to
deny all the allegations that she had read or heard said about her in
the media, especially internationally. With mere sleight of hand,
she dismissed the various tales of her shopping at Harrods, the
existence of foreign bank accounts and properties, her ferocious
temper and an alleged love affair with the governor of the Reserve
Bank of Zimbabwe, all without being seriously challenged by Tambo.

But the interview provided the world, and Zimbabweans in
particular, with a rare insight into the much-speculated-about lives
of the Mugabes. President Mugabe had traditionally denied Zim-

babwean journalists the opportunity for an open or meaningful interview. There was typically only the lacklustre 'President Mugabe's Birthday Interview', aired by the ZBC over the years on 21 February, his birthday.

While introducing her, Tambo describes Grace Mugabe as a woman of considerable beauty, who speaks frankly and openly with self-confidence and constant humour. 'To some in the Western media,' Tambo says, 'she has become "Disgrace" because of her alleged extravagance in the face of poverty. But for others who know her closer to home, she is a lady of energy, elegance and effervescence, whose charitable and sociable work has earned her the mantle of "Amazing Grace".'

Halfway through the interview, Tambo asks Mugabe's daughter, Bona, to tell her father on camera why 'she loves him so much'.

'Firstly,' Bona says, 'unlike some other fathers, you have always been there for me, whether emotionally or even financially. You are always taking care of us. I have everything I need. Not on one day have I ever had a problem with you. Your nature is what I love the most, I think. You are a very calm person as I have said before. You are very well educated. You are a strong person. You always fight for what you believe in and that's why I love you.'

'Is this some kind of joke?' a viewer asked after watching the interview on YouTube. 'This journalist is a bit sycophantic. What about the hundreds of thousands of Matabeles burned alive under Mugabe's orders? Isn't it time to face criminal proceedings? He's a bit old to be president and urinates himself in public frequently. Time to retire. It's undignified and very sad.'

As if in mitigation, another viewer commented, 'Grace Mugabe needs to do more of these interviews. It really would help change people's perceptions of her. It certainly has changed mine. Wow, who knew she was so eloquent and likeable?'

Grace Ntombizodwa Marufu was born of Zimbabwean migrant parents in Benoni, South Africa, on 23 July 1965, the fourth of five children. She grew up in this former gold-mining town until the age of five, when her mother, Idah Marufu, brought the children back to Zimbabwe, settling in the town of Enkeldoorn, now Chivhu in Mashonaland East Province. Grace's father remained behind in Benoni, working to support his family in Zimbabwe.

After attending primary school in Chivhu, she enrolled at Kriste Mambo Secondary School for Girls near the town of Rusape in Zimbabwe's eastern Manicaland Province. She got married at an early age to an Air Force of Zimbabwe officer, Stanley Goreraza, and the couple settled in Harare's township of Mufakose.

Grace enrolled for a secretarial training course and was offered a life-changing opportunity: a job in the typing pool of the Office of the President of Zimbabwe.

Her new boss, the president, and his ailing wife, First Lady Sally Mugabe, had tragically lost their only child, Nhamodzenyika, to malaria in 1966. Mugabe had been in political detention when this happened, while Sally was in Ghana, her home country. The colonial government in Salisbury refused to grant Mugabe permission to travel to Takoradi in Ghana to bury his only child, and Sally never conceived again. By the time that Grace was employed in the Office of the President, the First Lady survived by spending long periods on a dialysis machine for a kidney ailment. Her dialysis machine was the only one in the country then, or so it was whispered among the public.

Working in the typing pool and exposed to regular close encounters with the president, the young mother of one caught the eye of His Excellency. They soon fell in love, the affair no doubt blossoming when she was promoted, whether by design or by coincidence, to become his personal assistant. The office romance created problems in the modest Goreraza home in Mufakose.

Fidelis Kadziyanike, an air force friend of Goreraza's who now lives in Massachusetts, told me that Goreraza, who did not previously imbibe alcoholic beverages, had suddenly developed a drinking problem. Kadziyanike remembers him arriving at his apartment in the township of Glen Norah B and inviting him for an early morning drink in a neighbourhood shebeen – a drinking joint hosted in a private home. Shebeens were particularly popular in the City of Kings, Bulawayo, but they also have a modest presence in Harare.

At the shebeen, Goreraza surprised his friend when he ordered them drinks. Then he poured his heart out. Recently, Grace had taken to arriving home very late at night. She would be driven home in official cars, Goreraza said. The marriage was no longer the same. Soon it broke down irreparably and the two separated, with Grace retaining custody of the couple's young son, Russell.

The affair between Grace and the president soon yielded two offspring – a girl named Bona after Mugabe's mother, and a boy named Robert Jr – while the First Lady was still on dialysis.

Sally died in 1992. Four years later, Robert Mugabe and Grace Marufu, with their children in tow, were married in a ceremony presided over by Archbishop Patrick Fani Chakaipa of Harare, who was the first black Roman Catholic bishop in Zimbabwe. President Joaquim Chissano of Mozambique was the best man.

The wedding was a lavish affair of a magnitude never before witnessed in Zimbabwe, or elsewhere in Africa, for a head of state.

It was attended by virtually the entire leadership of the Southern African Development Community (SADC). Grace Mugabe was later to say that more than 40 000 guests had attended the function at Kutama, most of whom had not been invited.

Various versions of the story have since been told with amusement and gusto in Harare of the charming young typist who attracted the eye of the elderly and austere president of Zimbabwe. Meanwhile, many political pundits claim that Mugabe's worst error in political judgement was his 1996 decision to welcome into the State House a bride who was forty-one years his junior.

Speaking during the same interview with Dali Tambo, President Mugabe claimed that his first wife, Sally, was aware of his relationship with Grace before her death in 1992. Grace said that, on her part, she had no regrets over her liaison with Mugabe. She said that he was not unlike any other man, let alone a president, who had entered into a polygamous marriage. Polygamy is acceptable among the indigenous people of Zimbabwe and is widespread throughout the sub-Saharan region, she asserted.

'South African President Jacob Zuma has many wives,' Grace Mugabe has said in reaction to media criticism of her own romantic history. 'I admire him because he stands for what he wants.'

In fact, among the Shona people of Zimbabwe, of whom both Robert and Grace Mugabe are members, polygamy is an acceptable but not very widespread custom. Traditionally, a starving family would offer a young woman to a wealthy man to marry as an additional wife in return for food. Members of the Apostolic Faith group of churches are known to take on several wives, who are treated as a resource for labour to tend the fields, ideally providing several children each.

Over the past two to three decades, a new English phrase has crept into the Shona language and gained currency in Zimbabwe: 'small house'. This refers to an arrangement, especially in an urban setting, where a married man will take on another woman, often a divorcée or widow, and start a second family with her on the side. The abode of the second wife is known as the 'small house', with the woman herself being referred to in the same way. Occasionally, the man will go through the traditional procedure of paying lobola for his 'small house', often to the antagonism of his first wife. At the time of the president's affair with Grace while Sally was the First Lady, Grace would technically have been his 'small house'.

What is unlawful and totally unacceptable among the indigenous people of Zimbabwe, however, is a situation where a man has a sexual relationship with the wife of another man. Such practice is called *hupombwe* in chiShona and *ukuphinga* in siNdebele. Should the husband of the unfaithful woman discover the existence of the affair, he has recourse to reporting the matter to the chief. The paramour can be sentenced to payment of a fine in the form of a number of cattle to the aggrieved husband, with one of them being payable to the presiding chief.

In the case of the Goreraza household, the cuckolded young air force officer was in due course dispatched to China, no doubt by a presidential directive, for the ostensible purpose of enhancing his educational qualifications. On completion of his studies, he was posted to the Zimbabwean Embassy in Beijing as a defence attaché. While diplomats normally serve for four or five years in one station, at the time of writing, twenty-six years later, Goreraza was still stationed in Beijing.

Back in 1996, Ray Choto, then a reporter with *Horizon* magazine, investigated and duly reported that the president had officially paid lobola for his secretary. A picture of the couple's first-born child, Bona, accompanied the article. The arrival of Grace at the State House officially signalled not only the transformation of her status from 'small house' to First Lady but also the beginning of the meteoric rise of her political star. For some time, as she came to terms with her drastic transformation from Mrs Grace Goreraza to Zimbabwe's First Lady, not much was heard about the president's new wife.

Then the name Grace Mugabe started to be mentioned in ways that were not entirely befitting someone ensconced in the State House. A regular allegation was her extravagant spending habits, which struck a sharp contrast with the widespread poverty in Zimbabwe.

Yet, in her televised interview, the First Lady denied that she shopped lavishly and especially that she did so at Harrods in London. 'I do my own clothes and tie my own head scarf,' she said. 'They say I buy lavishly, but these are very cheap fabrics that I buy. The fabrics that I buy are not very expensive. Then I sit down to design my own clothes which I give to someone to make. Harrods is one place where I have never bought an outfit from.'

While it may be true that quite a number of Grace Mugabe's dresses include African-designed attire, she has appeared at many special and official functions while wearing very expensive-looking and elegant designer outfits. Dali Tambo could have easily pinned her down on this had he wished to do so.

Nevertheless, gossip continued to surround the image of the First Lady. Her life in the State House was, from quite early in her marriage to President Mugabe, surrounded by rumours of her having extramarital affairs with various high-profile men in the capital city. While some of these allegations have arisen from multiple sources – from social media on the internet to tabloid newspapers on the street corners of Harare – she has never taken any robust action for defamation. As a matter of routine, none of the newspapers involved has offered her any opportunity to respond to or comment on the allegations made against her, as the ethical practice of journalism requires.

But Tambo did ask the First Lady to address one particular issue – that of her alleged liaison with the Reserve Bank of Zimbabwe governor Gideon Gono, who was the first official in Mugabe's inner circle to be romantically linked to the president's wife.

She denied the allegation vehemently. 'No please, no please!' she shouted. 'It's not right. It's not nice. He is the governor of the Reserve Bank of Zimbabwe. The places they were saying we have gone to, I have never been to those places, in South Africa, in Malaysia or in any other countries.'

The First Lady said that the only occasion she had travelled on the same plane with the governor was when she and the president had visited the island of Langkawi, off the coast of Malaysia, to attend a Smart Partnership conference.

Turning to her relationship with her husband, Grace Mugabe declared, 'We are a happy couple. We are very close. We get along very well. I know he trusts me.'

But the persistent rumours would not go away. And, in due course, the paternity of her sons, Robert Jr and Chatunga Bellarmine, started to be attributed to some of the men who were said to be her lovers. Pictures of the boys matched against their alleged fathers went viral on social media.

One of the First Lady's purported paramours, Peter Pamire, a young and handsome upcoming businessperson and black-empower-ment militant, died in a horrific traffic accident on his way from the Harare airport after a trip to Johannesburg in 1996. He report-edly lost control of his vehicle, which rolled several times. This was the same year that Grace Mugabe married President Mugabe. Alle-gations that Pamire had been shot dead before his SUV crashed were never conclusively investigated, even after one CIO agent told *New Zimbabwe*, an online news publication, that he was part of a team that had been hired to assassinate Pamire.

The agent, identified by *New Zimbabwe* as Agent K, told the website's editor, Mduduzi Mathuthu, 'I couldn't live with the fact that I was party to a murder of an innocent man directly authorized by President Mugabe. I am doing this for posterity.' However, even this testimony was not sufficient to prompt the police to investi-gate the alleged murder. Many years later, a composite picture of Pamire and Robert Mugabe Jr was posted on social media. Many who saw the image were struck by the uncanny resemblance between the two.

Another composite image also went viral; this one featured the younger Mugabe son, Chatunga Bellarmine, as matched with the commissioner general of police Dr Augustine Chihuri. Again, there appeared to be unanimity that the two were like father and son.

The most sensational link between Grace Mugabe and a rumoured paramour was the one involving James Makamba, a former disc jockey turned wealthy businessperson and small-time politician. He was the business partner of Solomon Mujuru, who had been the first commander of the ZNA at independence and who had become a wealthy and politically powerful farmer and businessperson on retirement from the ZDF.

During a crackdown on dozens of businesspeople alleged to have externalised foreign currency, Makamba was arrested in February 2004 and charged with violation of Zimbabwe's Exchange Control Act. After he was subsequently arrested on two further occasions, he was put on trial in the magistrates' court and in the High Court of Zimbabwe. The state charged him with allegedly externalising £3.7 million, US$2.1 million and R15 million. He was acquitted on all three charges, but he spent a significant amount of time in custody, being denied bail on thirteen occasions. In 2005, Makamba skipped bail and fled into self-imposed exile, initially in South Africa and later in the UK.

On 29 February 2004, Dr Ibbo Joseph Mandaza's newspaper, the *Sunday Mirror*, published a scathing article that was critical of the government's heavy-handed treatment of Makamba's case. The piece was penned by Tendai Dumbutshena, who is the son of Zimbabwe's first indigenous chief justice, Enoch Dumbutshena, and a friend of Makamba's. Justice Dumbutshena was another of Mugabe's targets of relentless animosity. In the article, Tendai wrote the following:

Over the years, it has been common knowledge in ruling party circles that the President loathes Makamba for reasons that only he knows. Recent events have confirmed this. On the eve of his 80th birthday the President gave an interview on what was supposed to be a happy occasion. This did not stop him from launching a vitriolic attack against Makamba, calling him an underling of Tiny Rowland.

For the benefit of young readers, Rowland was the CEO and founder of the London-based Lonrho multinational conglomerate.

Makamba is not a violent man. He has no previous convictions. All this is known to the people who head the police, CIO and defence forces. As stated above, many of these people can justifiably be considered friends. Police Commissioner Augustine Chihuri has a warm personal relationship with Makamba. It is therefore impossible to believe the crude paramilitary operation to arrest Makamba was his brainchild. He was simply obeying orders. These orders were given to the public broadcaster to tell the multitudes that Makamba's whereabouts had to be divulged as he constituted a moral danger to national security.

Dumbutshena suggests that there might have been a time, in the 1980s, when the ideological differences between the capitalist Makamba and the socialist Mugabe would have caused conflict. But, he writes, 'The Marxist-Leninist one-party project was abandoned long ago', and within ZANU-PF 'a crude form of capitalist accumulation is now the dominant ethos'. He continues:

> It cannot be true, as suggested by some self-proclaimed analysts, that Makamba is being victimized for political reasons. To be brutally honest, politically Makamba is inconsequential. Like many in ZANU-PF and government with lofty titles, he is expendable fodder. He poses no threat to anyone. The idea that President Mugabe sees Makamba as some political threat is patently ludicrous.
>
> If Makamba has committed crimes, he must face the music. The rule of law must, however, prevail. The presumption of innocence must prevail. Undue pressure on the judiciary by

an all-powerful Head of State to convict must cease. This is personal hatred gone too far. It must stop forthwith.

After publication of Dumbutshena's article, commentators in Harare began to offer their own answers. The usual analysts claimed that Makamba's ordeal had nothing to do with any perception by Mugabe that Makamba was a political threat to the presidency, or with any alleged breach of law through the externalisation of foreign currency. Otherwise, they argued, the law would have been allowed to take its course.

The real cause of Makamba's arrest – or so it was strongly rumoured on social media – was the alleged love affair between him and Grace Mugabe. People in the corridors of power said that the relationship had become common knowledge at the highest levels of ZANU-PF and government. This was a euphemism for the president of the land.

Although the veracity of these detailed allegations may never be substantiated, they nonetheless undermined the First Lady's moral standing while they lasted and dented the credibility and stature of her husband. Grace Mugabe herself suggests that the attacks on her morality reached a crescendo at the time of the widely condemned land invasions in 2000. She suggests that this was a strategy by her husband's many detractors to discredit him at a time when he was incurring the wrath of the Western world.

In a comment on Grace Mugabe's alleged affairs and their effect on the government, the chairperson of the ZNLWVA, Chris Mutsvangwa – who was a former minister in the Mugabe regime – coined the term 'First Boyfriends'. 'You now have a pseudo administration that is exclusively led by a bunch of "First Boyfriends" who are neither equipped nor qualified to be in such positions,' he said, speaking while in Johannesburg on 13 November 2017, two days before Mugabe's downfall.

Mutsvangwa suggested that the status of governance in the Mugabe administration had deteriorated to the extent that just as officials could be dismissed for reasons other than their performance, they could also be appointed to high office on nepotistic grounds. Quite often, it only became apparent that certain officials were related to the First Family when Mugabe revealed details of their relationship in a eulogy after their death.

While Mutsvangwa's theory of 'First Boyfriends' may have been hyperbolic, it was generally accepted that nepotism, corruption and general mismanagement were some of the leading causes in Zimbabwe's sustained economic and political crises.

6

Origins of
ZANU-PF factionalism

*'This [factionalism] is due to the unresolved consequences
of the increasingly topical yet hitherto undefined Tsholotsho
Declaration of November 18, 2004, whose ghost is now
haunting Zanu PF succession politics.'*
— Professor Jonathan Nathaniel Moyo, 2004

At ZANU-PF's December 2016 elective congress, President Mugabe was confirmed as its official presidential candidate in the forthcoming 2018 harmonised elections.

Addressing concerns now routinely voiced about her husband's advanced age, First Lady Grace Mugabe assured the nation that if Mugabe secured another term as president, he would even be wheeled to the swearing-in ceremony if necessary. If that victory had come to pass, Mugabe would have been ninety-nine by the end of his ninth term as Zimbabwe's head of state. To ensure continuity in the event of his death, Grace had gone so far as to assure the shocked nation that her husband would continue to serve as president even from the confines of his tomb at the National Heroes' Acre.

Many theories have been put forward by analysts and observers, as well as by genuinely concerned Zimbabweans, as to why President

Mugabe seemed motivated by a consummate desire to remain in office in perpetuity – particularly since it became patently clear during the last two decades of his tenure that he remained in office against the will of the majority of the country's citizens. Amid the variety of offered opinions, some have been realistic, while others have been quite outlandish.

A number of theorists have suggested that Mugabe is imbued with such arrogance that he seems to genuinely believe that he is God's own gift to Zimbabwe, and that without him the country is destined to flounder or come to some calamity. His continued occupancy of the State House was therefore perhaps seen by Mugabe as a necessary ingredient for Zimbabwe's well-being.

Another theory is that, having perceived that Zimbabwe was no longer the success story that had been expected in the early days of independence and that his own image had become tarnished by Gukurahundi, corruption and the country's economic decline, Mugabe was seized by a state of denial. He became determined to extend his tenure, while hoping against hope that he would be able to revive Zimbabwe's fortunes and bring about a period of recovery. That way, his eventual departure would not be embroiled in total ignominy.

Whichever view is more accurate, the fact remains that Mugabe's presidency became deeply problematic in terms of his failing to put in place a clearly defined line of succession in the event of his death, incapacitation or removal from office. The absence of such an arrangement, whether by design or default amid concerns about the president's advanced age, was the direct cause of the factionalism that bedevilled ZANU-PF's politics and which ultimately led to Mugabe's precipitous removal from power.

Towards the end of his reign, however, factionalism was more likely a direct result of the machinations of a coterie of ZANU-PF politicians that established itself around the First Lady, united by a singular determination to install her in the position of vice president of the party as a prelude to her accession to the office of president of Zimbabwe.

The concomitant conflict was certainly exacerbated by Zimbabwe's polarised media, especially the print press, which quite clearly delighted in fuelling the feuds between the party's rival divisions. And quite often, articles were published whose text bore little resemblance to the sensational headlines under which they appeared.

Strictly speaking, though, the fierce factional fighting within ZANU-PF can be traced back to the so-called Tsholotsho Declaration in November 2004. This conspiracy involved several high-ranking officials from the party's various provinces, the most prominent among them being Jonathan Moyo, who was the minister of information and publicity and also the legislator for the Tsholotsho North constituency.

The internal conflict that culminated in the unsigned Tsholotsho Declaration surfaced in the most unlikely of places: the small administrative and business centre of Tsholotsho, which is about 100 kilometres north-west of Bulawayo in the province of Matabeleland North. While Mugabe had ostensibly remained secure in his seat of power as president and first secretary of ZANU-PF, as well as in his position as president of Zimbabwe, undercurrents of discontent with his leadership had festered for at least thirteen years before his forced resignation.

In fact, the roots of this discord perhaps go back to the early years of independence, when Mugabe became obsessed with the desire to remain president for life through the creation of a one-party system of government, allowing him to exercise autocratic power as an unchallenged leader. This dream of his was anchored in the assumption that ZANU-PF would remain a united and homogeneous political entity, supporting and protecting his power indefinitely.

Indeed, were it not for two unrelated dynamics, Mugabe might truly have become president for life. One is that Mugabe has enjoyed an exceedingly long and unusually healthy life, which meant that he lived for decades past the usual point of retirement and became to old to remain in office. The second factor that militated against Mugabe's wish for lifelong sovereignty is the fact that, far from his own political expectations, ZANU-PF was not always cohesive, as the growing factionalism within the party would demonstrate.

Mugabe's intention to remain in office until death was reinforced over the years by a wish to avert any negative consequences of his clearly growing unpopularity. He started to alienate himself from the people in 1987, when he amended the Constitution and abolished the office of prime minister while creating the executive presidency. This was followed by his signing of the controversial Unity Accord with his long-term rival Joshua Nkomo, the leader of PF-ZAPU. Technically, Mugabe had paved the way for a one-party state.

The former-secretary general of ZANU-PF, Edgar Tekere, who was a firebrand politician and who had been Mugabe's companion as they crossed the border to join the liberation struggle in Mozambique in 1975, was disparaging of Mugabe's professed Marxist–Leninist ideological trappings. Tekere suggested that his companion was merely a socialist of convenience. It would appear that Mugabe at heart was a capitalist, using doctrinaire Marxist–

Leninist demagoguery to facilitate his aspiration to establish a one-party state in order to conceal his strategy to remain in office permanently. With the passage of time, this would protect him from condemnation and retribution for multiple acts of alleged wrongdoing.

Tekere gave the following explanation: 'I want to single out one man in particular who spoilt Mugabe – Rugare Gumbo ... He had been in charge of publicity in the Chitepo-led external group before Mugabe left Rhodesia. He was a very effective propagandist, an ideologue. He began preaching Marxism. Mugabe liked the sound of this ideology, and before long, he had completely fallen for it and begun to sing the Marxism/Leninism song. But that's all it was – rhetoric. There was no genuine vision or belief behind it.'

Nevertheless, the ZANU-PF congress in December 1989 adopted a document that expressed the party's aim 'to establish and sustain a socialist society guided by Marxist–Leninist principles but firmly based on our historical, cultural and social experience and to create conditions for economic independence, increased productivity and equitable distribution of the wealth of the nation'.

On that note, the ZANU-PF congress literally granted Mugabe free rein to transform Zimbabwe into a socialist one-party state. While Zimbabwe remained in principle a Western-style democracy, as guaranteed by the Constitution for the first ten years of the country's independence, in practice, after that grace period, Mugabe would have been able to use a two-thirds majority in Parliament to ban opposition parties and establish a single-party state, if he so wished.

But this would have multiplied the number of Mugabe's problems and enemies, both in Zimbabwe and in Western democracies.

His greatest achievement in pursuing more balanced political relations was the signing of the Unity Accord with Nkomo's PF-ZAPU. By doing so, however, ZANU-PF effectively emasculated its only viable opponent. In due course, the 1990 harmonised elections became the first polls to be contested under the amended Constitution of 1987, which established the elected executive presidency while abolishing the senate.

While ZANU-PF secured a total of 117 of the 120 elected seats in Parliament, Mugabe himself garnered 83 per cent of the popular vote in the presidential election in comparison with his rival Edgar Tekere's 16.95 per cent. By the 1996 presidential election, Mugabe had increased his majority to an overwhelming 92.76 per cent, with Abel Muzorewa of the United Parties and Ndabaningi Sithole of ZANU-Ndonga trailing far behind him with a paltry 4.80 per cent and 2.44 per cent, respectively.

At that stage, the opposition had effectively been defused. What remained was for Mugabe to buttress his domination over his own party, the now enlarged ZANU-PF. This was not an immensely difficult assignment to undertake. By the new millennium, Mugabe had become a much-dreaded leader within ZANU-PF. Although a new opposition party, the MDC of Morgan Tsvangirai, had emerged in September 1999 to become a serious threat, Mugabe still held sway within his own party. More tellingly, few if any ZANU-PF politicians of substance crossed the floor to join the MDC, as would have been expected on the emergence of a new political organisation of substance.

Mugabe had become effectively entrenched in his internally unchallenged position as leader of ZANU-PF. But the emergence of the MDC as a viable opposition party, given the inroads that it had made during the 2000 parliamentary election and the 2002 presidential election, seriously dented the lustre of Mugabe's aura of invincibility. At his first showing, Tsvangirai reduced Mugabe's majority from 92.76 per cent in 1996 to 56.2 per cent in 2002, while the opposition leader garnered an impressive 42 per cent of the ballots cast.

Mugabe was seventy-eight years old by 2002, and his advanced age was becoming a matter of public concern, even within his own ZANU-PF. Two years later, in 2004, the increasing rumblings of discontent escalated to become a major political crisis, sparked by the controversial Tsholotsho Declaration. Following the death of Vice President Simon Muzenda in 2003, ZANU-PF was plunged into an unprecedented hive of succession-related activity. Two distinct factions eventually emerged, each seeking to identify a replacement for the position left vacant by the deceased vice president. It was in the context of this battle to replace Muzenda that the Tsholotsho Declaration precipitated an internal political crisis that resulted in an extended period of factionalism within the party.

The Tsholotsho Declaration was an unwritten agreement that emerged from a meeting in a Bulawayo hotel by senior party officials belonging to a faction of ZANU-PF. The party officials had initially attended a speech day and prize-giving ceremony that day at the invitation of Jonathan Moyo at Dinyane Secondary School in Tsholotsho. While Moyo made a feeble attempt to cast the attendance of so many ZANU-PF heavyweights at such a function in rural Tsholotsho in the mould of regular support for a school event, the large turnout of politicians so far away from their own constituencies left observers in no doubt that there was something unusual happening.

Six of the ten ZANU-PF provincial chairs, as well as some members of the party's Politburo and Central Committee, a good number of the party's legislators, and members of the powerful war veterans' group, attended a meeting convened at the school that day. From there they adjourned to Bulawayo, where deliberations continued late into the night. By the time the meeting terminated, an agreement had allegedly been reached.

Moyo was a key player in the deliberations leading to the Tsholotsho Declaration. He had been at pains to explain that the agreement was merely verbal, with nothing committed to writing, as would be expected in such circumstances.

In an article titled 'Tsholotsho saga: The untold story', published on 17 December 2004 in the *Zimbabwe Independent*, Moyo made reference to 'the unresolved consequences of the increasingly topical yet hitherto undefined Tsholotsho Declaration of November 18, 2004, whose ghost is now haunting Zanu PF succession politics'. The main feature of the agreement was a strategy to install Emmerson Dambudzo Mnangagwa, then minister of defence, in the presidium as a successor to Simon Muzenda.

In terms of the controversial agreement, Mnangagwa was to become the vice president and eventually assume the presidency of both ZANU-PF and Zimbabwe. The meeting was held ahead of a key ZANU-PF elective congress in December 2004. While Mnangagwa had secured the support of six of the country's ten provinces *in absentia*, he was outmanoeuvred by Mugabe. Interpreting the events surrounding the Tsholotsho Declaration as a challenge to his position, Mugabe used a Politburo meeting to unconstitutionally amend the party's constitution to ensure that one of the party's two vice presidents was always a woman. Because the other vice president at the time was former PF-ZAPU's Joseph

Msika, who was in office from 1999 to 2009, Mugabe's shrewd move saw Joice Teurai Ropa Mujuru emerge as vice president at the December 2004 ZANU-PF congress. She was, in fact, the first woman ever to hold the position in Zimbabwe.

Mnangagwa was effectively left hanging high and dry, and the seeds were sown for the factionalism that was to afflict ZANU-PF for the next thirteen years. It is pertinent to note that the vice presidency on the former PF-ZAPU side of ZANU-PF was apparently better managed than on the ZANU-PF side of the dual vice presidency. This was because the former PF-ZAPU vice presidents were not expected to rise to become president and first secretary of ZANU-PF and president of Zimbabwe itself thereafter. The Unity Accord appears to have placed a ceiling, including in the case of Joshua Nkomo himself, on the presidential ambitions of former PF-ZAPU politicians. Through some unwritten law, Joseph Msika, John Nkomo and Phelekezela Mphoko all served as vice presidents without arousing widespread expectations that they would one day succeed Mugabe as president of the country.

It was on the former ZANU-PF side of the presidential succession that Mugabe had cause for concern or anxiety, especially after the death of his loyal deputy in the party, Simon Muzenda. Muzenda's discernible docility and unquestionable loyalty had lulled Mugabe into a sense of security and invincibility. With Muzenda's passing in 2003, Mnangagwa would have been the natural successor to Mugabe, as he was generally regarded as the president's favoured heir. Mnangagwa, however, clashed with the former ZNA commander Solomon Mujuru, who had emerged as a powerful force within the tumult of ZANU-PF succession politics.

The conflict between Mujuru and Mnangagwa had rather catastrophic consequences for the rest of ZANU-PF and, to some extent, the country. It arose when Mujuru, then a successful business entrepreneur, attempted to buy into the multibillion-dollar Zimbabwe Mining and Smelting Company, an operation in the Midlands town of Kwekwe, where Mnangagwa was regarded in ZANU-PF circles as a godfather.

However, the Mujuru faction, which had the tacit support of the president and the First Lady, emerged as the stronger of the two rival groups. Mnangagwa's position was further weakened when the six provincial chairs who had backed him at Tsholotsho – one of whom was Jonathan Moyo – were expelled from the party.

As intra-party rivalries worsened, Solomon Mujuru began to flex his muscles. This was especially so after the establishment of the GNU in 2009, when there was a widely held expectation that the Mujuru faction would align with the MDC in Parliament in order to create a Joice Mujuru–Tsvangirai alliance in the run-up to the 2013 elections. Overall, Solomon Mujuru's prospects were good. His spouse was vice president. He enjoyed support from the armed forces, and he had credibility among MPs and the Zimbabwean public at large. He also commanded respect, some of it grudging, within the ranks of the business community. The retired general had also built a reputation as being one of the only officials with the courage to stand up to Mugabe in Politburo meetings and to have openly urged Mugabe, on one occasion, to step down on account of his advanced age. With such solid credentials on the part of the Mujuru faction, and the massive electoral support demonstrated by Tsvangirai's MDC-T in 2008, when Tsvangirai defeated Mugabe in the presidential election, the marriage between Mujuru and Tsvangirai sounded like one made in heaven.

The daily newspaper *NewsDay* reported in an article published on 16 August 2011 that since recent encounters, Mujuru and Mnangagwa 'have been at crossroads which led to them leading opposing factions in Zanu PF. The factions are locked in a bitter fight of attrition to succeed the ailing and ageing Mugabe.'

According to the article, the retired general wanted his wife, Vice President Joice Mujuru, to succeed Mugabe, while the other faction was pushing for the defence minister to take over from the then eighty-seven-year-old president.

Amid the disputes, Mugabe had grown to regard the Mujurus as potential rivals for power. It was difficult for him to consider that they could be relied upon to preserve his vast wealth if he ever left office, especially since Solomon had openly urged Mugabe to step down from the presidency.

The deterioration in their relationship was further aggravated by Grace Mugabe, who increasingly viewed Joice and Solomon Mujuru not only as competitors for political power but also – because of Solomon's stake in diamond dealings in the Marange diamond fields in Manicaland and elsewhere – as major threats to her own interests in the country's profitable diamond-mining operations.

The *Zimbabwe Daily* published a report on 30 July 2010 suggesting that the First Lady, together with the Zimbabwe Mining Development Corporation, had a substantial interest in Mbada Diamonds, one of the companies that were clandestinely awarded mining rights at Chiadzwa by Obert Mpofu, the minister of mines in the Mugabe government.

All of these competing financial and political motives only deepened the factional rifts within Zimbabwe's ruling party.

Nevertheless, while it is indisputable that Mugabe's wish was to remain in office for life, this isn't the same as desiring to have no successor at all. Mugabe may not have laid out a clear succession plan, but he never expressed that none among his lieutenants should succeed him after his death. The impression that he held this stance was most likely bolstered by the First Lady, whose ambition to succeed her husband as president would ultimately rely on exploiting the party's factionalism to its breaking point.

7

Mujuru's death: Accident or assassination?

'In Geneva we burnt down a hotel and it was Mujuru again.'
— Robert Mugabe, 2018

On 15 August 2011, a tragic incident threw Zimbabwe into turmoil and shook the Mugabe presidency to its roots. This was the sudden death of Solomon Mujuru in circumstances that have defied conclusive investigation and fuelled speculation in the years since.

Aged sixty-two at the time of his death, Mujuru perished in a fire that was as furious as it is mysterious at his Alamein Farm in Beatrice, sixty kilometres south of Harare. He is said to have been alone in his car when he arrived home at around 8 p.m. on that fateful night.

Mujuru, known as Rex Nhongo during the liberation war, was the first commander of the ZNA after independence, and he was widely regarded subsequently as one of the most feared men in Zimbabwean politics. His wife, Joice, was also a recognised war hero and was one of Mugabe's closest allies in ZANU-PF. Yet despite her excellent credentials, the path of her political career was assisted by Solomon Mujuru's influence. This included her ascendancy to the vice presidency of ZANU-PF and government in 2004, when she was pitted against the powerful defence minister Emmerson Mnangagwa, following the death of former vice president Simon Muzenda in 2003.

In the cut-throat succession politics of the time, Solomon Mujuru – who was widely regarded as a kingmaker in ZANU-PF, capable of guiding ambitious politicians to the top of the party – was not a force to be taken lightly.

During the war of liberation, Mujuru and the legendary guerrilla Josiah Tongogara had led the ZANLA military wing of ZANU, which was based in Mozambique. After Mujuru petitioned the ZANLA fighters to accept Mugabe as the leader of ZANU in 1976, he was appointed the following year as military chief of ZIPA, which was a merger of the ZIPRA forces of Joshua Nkomo's ZAPU and the ZANLA cadres of Mugabe's ZANU. Between 1976 and 1979, Mujuru was placed in charge of all ZANLA military operations inside Rhodesia, including the deployment of cadres and their infiltration into war zones.

In the absence of General Tongogara, who had died in what some viewed as a mysterious car crash in Mozambique just after the Lancaster House Agreement, Mujuru emerged on return to Rhodesia as the top ZANLA officer, and he played a key role in merging ZANLA, Nkomo's ZIPRA guerrilla insurgents, and the Rhodesian Security Forces (whom the rebel armies had engaged in battle throughout the 1970s) into one united army, the ZNA.

In 1980, during the ceasefire, Mujuru was in charge of the demobilisation of the ZANLA guerrillas at the countrywide assembly points. It was widely rumoured that he made much of his early wealth during this process. He travelled around the country with trunks full of cash to disburse among the returning guerrillas. There was little accounting for the millions of dollars in motion, and Mujuru quickly gained a reputation as being a law unto himself.

Taking over from General Peter Walls, commander of the Rhodesian Army, Mujuru became one of the most influential and feared figures in the new Zimbabwe.

As army chief, he was rumoured to have made a fortune from bribes and kickbacks on lucrative contracts, construction projects, and the acquisition of military equipment and vehicles. This often happened openly, supposedly with the knowledge and tacit blessings of President Mugabe. One such alleged case was the importation of a huge consignment of ninety Cascavel armoured cars from Brazil in the early 1980s. The army clearly offered magnificent opportunities for self-enrichment, and General Mujuru seems to have seized them with determination.

After he retired from the ZNA, he partnered with James Makamba, a radio DJ in Harare in the years leading up to independence, and established a company called Thurlow and Company (Pvt) Limited, which acquired substantial pieces of choice real estate in the Mashonaland Central mining and agricultural town of Bindura. Mujuru soon became the owner of a hotel, multiple farms (including Alamein Farm, which he seized from Guy Watson-Smith during the controversial fast-track land-reform programme of the early 2000s), a chain of supermarkets and several residential properties. His ventures were so successful that he quickly built up a vast business empire across many key sectors of the economy, including a 20 per cent stake in the River Ranch diamond mine.

Makamba, on the other hand, had made his break when Air Zimbabwe purchased its first Boeing 767, one of a new generation of wide-bodied twin-engine jet aircraft, in 1988. He earned millions in commission. Makamba was to flee from Zimbabwe when he was targeted by President Mugabe on suspicion that he'd had an affair with the First Lady. He went into exile, first in the UK and later nearer home, in Johannesburg, South Africa. He returned to Zimbabwe only after Mugabe's fall from power in late 2017.

During the intervening years, Mujuru took advantage of his power and influence and ventured into serious politics. He was duly elected as the MP for the Chikomba constituency in Mashonaland East Province on a ZANU-PF ticket in 1994.

A decade later, in 2004, Joice Mujuru would rise to become the vice president of Zimbabwe, whereas her husband had decided to retire from public life in 2000. It is pertinent to note that despite the war of words that would erupt between Vice President Joice Mujuru and First Lady Grace Mugabe, both Solomon and Grace hailed from the same Chikomba District, which wielded much power at the time. Charles Utete, the former chief secretary in the Office of the President and Cabinet, was also from Chikomba and could have used his influence, even after retirement, to broker a peace deal between them.

Politically, Solomon Mujuru had become so powerful that in 2008 he was linked to the formation of a new political party that was being launched by the former minister of finance Dr Simba Makoni. There was widespread speculation that Mujuru and another ZANU-PF stalwart, Dumiso Dabengwa, a former top PF-ZAPU official, were lending Makoni crucial support behind the scenes before coming out publicly as heavyweights of the proposed Mavambo-Kusile-Dawn political outfit.

The expected announcements never took place. By that time, Joice Mujuru was in her fifth year as vice president. But it had become common knowledge that the retired general was anxious to see the end of Mugabe's reign and that his preference was for Simba Makoni to take over. Among the many rumours circulated about Mujuru was one that he had confronted Mugabe at the State House and apparently told the president to his face that he must step down and make way for fresh blood.

At that time, Joice was not a big factor in the Mujuru camp. In fact, her husband was convinced that she was not presidential material. In addition, the Mujuru marriage had other factors straining it, with Solomon given to barely concealed acts of infidelity. The fact that he died while alone in the Beatrice farmhouse is a pointer in this direction.

The awful nature of this incident was the cause of many conspiracy theories. It was difficult for many people to accept that Mujuru, a respected war hero who was leading a faction in the battle to determine Mugabe's successor, could die in a simple house fire.

Mugabe himself unwittingly fuelled this speculation when he read Mujuru's obituary at the National Heroes' Acre: 'It is hard to imagine that such a glorious soldier died in such an inglorious way, so uneventfully. But this is how God willed it and we cannot do anything about it, except to grieve, to ask so many questions and finally accept his demise even though it will always hurt.'

With that comment, Harare's rumour mill went instantly into overdrive. This peculiar phenomenon thrived on the Mugabe government's clampdown on the free flow of information, which was compounded by the failure of the country's polarised press to undertake serious investigations. Instead of probing into important events in a meaningful way, journalists often resorted to pure speculation.

'Who killed Solomon Mujuru?' a front-page headline in *The*

Zimbabwean asked on 8 April 2015, almost four years after his death. Newspaper readers normally expect journalists to provide them with insights into such matters of national interest. Yet the attached article was rather on the unceremonious dismissal of Joice Mujuru from her position as vice president of Zimbabwe in December 2014.

Several factors should have influenced the thinking of those who were genuinely anxious (or, at least, professionally obligated) to unravel the circumstances surrounding Solomon Mujuru's death. While circumstantial evidence might have pointed in the direction of an assassination, investigators – both police officers and journalists – are trained to maintain an open mind, without rushing to preconceived conclusions, and to desist from being influenced by public opinion. Was Mujuru's death an assassination, a suicide or a genuine accident? Linked to these possibilities is the further question of whether he was drunk or coherent at the time of his death. Mujuru's maid, from whom he had collected keys for the house when he realised that he had left his own set behind in Harare, made an interesting disclosure. She said that Mujuru had told her that he had considered sleeping in his car, as she claimed he occasionally did, to avoid driving the distance to the maid's quarters.

Witnesses told police inquirers and the inquest that Mujuru had stopped over at the Beatrice Country Club, as was his customary practice on his way to the farm, often late at night. He is reported to have drunk four Scotch whiskies.

It is common knowledge among those familiar with the drinking habits of top officials in the upper echelons of ZANU-PF and government, as well as those of the captains of the corporate world, that it is generally considered *infra dig* among them to order only a single tot of Johnnie Walker Blue Label or Glenfiddich single malt or whatever their favourite choice may be. In certain circles, the status of one's position in Harare is measured by the age of the double tot of single malt that one orders at the bar at the Sports Club or at the Meikles or Rainbow Towers Hotel. While Mugabe's Zimbabwe was rated as a poor Third World nation, the reality is that expensive whiskies flow like water in Harare, as top decision-makers regularly discuss the hopeless state of the economy or other such matters.

On the night of Mujuru's death, if he had ordered four doubles of whisky, he would have consumed a total of eight single tots before driving home to retire for the night. There is also no guarantee that the four drinks he had at the Beatrice Country Club were his only intake of alcohol that Monday.

Evidence at hand, which was circulated as being relevant to the events surrounding the incident but which wasn't played up during police investigations or during the inquest, suggested that Mujuru had visited a favourite drinking joint of his, the Captain's Pavilion of the famous Harare Sports Club, on Sunday 14 August 2011. The reason for Mujuru's presence at the club that afternoon was to watch the second One Day International of the Bangladesh cricket tour of Zimbabwe.

Among the notable people there who chatted with Mujuru were the chair of the club, Muchadeyi Ashton Masunda, who was mayor of Harare and former CEO of Associated Newspapers, the publisher of the *Daily News*; local government minister Saviour Kasukuwere; and Peter Farai Chingoka, chair of Cricket Zimbabwe. I make reference to them only in the context of the importance subsequently attached to Mujuru's drink in the Captain's Pavilion that day.

Unfortunately, there was a rush on the part of the Mujuru family

– as well as by the press, to some extent – to claim that Solomon Mujuru had been assassinated. Despite the fact that nobody could offer a shred of evidence to support this assumption, especially in terms of identifying a motive or suspect, there was a swift readiness to cast the blame on President Mugabe. Typical of the adversarial and polarised positions of the Zimbabwe media, government-aligned news outlets were quick to characterise Mujuru's death as an accident, while the privately owned press appeared keen to convince the public that Mujuru had been assassinated.

Neither side undertook to investigate the incident thoroughly or to present the public with the outcome of any conclusive inquiry. Even the foreign media presented divergent views of how Mujuru's death had occurred.

Reuters, an international news agency headquartered in London, reported on 16 August 2011, the day after Mujuru's death was discovered, that the retired general had apparently died in a fire accident. 'There was no suggestion either by authorities or Mujuru's family that the fire was anything but an accident,' the report concluded.

On the other hand, Guy Watson-Smith, the owner of Alamein Farm until his unceremonious eviction by Mujuru's men back in 2001, told Zimbabwean journalist Violet Gonda of Voice of America's *Studio 7* in Washington D.C., that it was 'improbable' that Mujuru's death in the fourteen-roomed house could have been an accident. 'The main bedroom where I understand he may finally have been found has three exit doors just from that one bedroom alone, plus four double windows,' he said. 'So it seemed to me improbable that anybody could be trapped in such an open home.'

But as Watson-Smith started to narrate some interesting details about the layout of the farm employees' compound in relation to the main farmhouse, Gonda diverted him with a question regarding Watson-Smith's personal experience at the time of the farm's invasion by Mujuru's men ten years back.

Also on 16 August 2011, the BBC quoted an unidentified relative of Mujuru as saying, 'It began when the general was alone. Guards noticed plumes of smoke and called the maid.' According to this version of events, the guards said that they had tried to get into the house but that the flames were so fierce they couldn't enter. The BBC didn't explain why the guards' instinctive reactions were to call the maid from her quarters, which were some distance away, on discovering that Mujuru's house was on fire. Presumably the maid had been sleeping in her own quarters in the workers' compound.

Andrew Meldrum, a seasoned journalist reporting for *GlobalPost,* wrote the following: 'Adding further fuel to the controversy, Zimbabwean Finance Minister Tendai Biti, who is a member of [Morgan] Tsvangirai's MDC, charged that Mujuru's death "has Zanu-PF's fingerprints on it".' Biti suggested that Mujuru was 'killed in an internecine war within Zanu-PF over who will succeed Mugabe'.

Meldrum didn't ask Biti to offer any reasons to support this theory, most likely because the minister's hypothesis was, in essence, one that any MDC politician at the time would have easily volunteered in order to discredit their rival, ZANU-PF. In any case, Biti's value as a source of credible information on Solomon Mujuru's death in the middle of the night some sixty kilometres outside of Harare was also not explained. In fact, Biti had been nowhere near the farm before assuming his role as a commentator.

Eleven days later, Peta Thornycroft and Aislinn Laing, Johannesburg-based correspondents for the London newspaper *The Telegraph,* filed a report on 27 August, quoting an unidentified politician: "'The feeling across the country, wherever you go, whoever you talk to, is that he was murdered," said one senior Zimbabwean politition. "No one wants to talk about this in public because there is so much tension.'"

Amid all this speculation about the likely cause of Mujuru's death, a Facebook post by Elliot Pfebve, a Zimbabwean politician better known as an MDC-T activist, provides a revealing perspective on the matter. Not only did Pfebve's post declare two cabinet ministers, Saviour Kasukuwere and Supa Collins Mandiwanzira, to be the last two people to interact with the retired general before his death, but it also categorically pinned Mujuru's death on at least Kasukuwere.

Pfebve's post, which brought the fatal incident forward to the early hours of Monday morning, a full day before it actually happened, was reproduced in full by Shakespeare Muzavazi of the *Zimbabwe News Network*. The following is Pfebve's Facebook post, as captured by Muzavazi and quoted here as it serves to provide evidence that after Mujuru's death, some journalists and members of the public made a habit of presenting idle speculation as the verified truth:

Saviour Kasukuwere and Supa Mandiwanzira were the last two people who last saw General Mujuru, I can reveal.

General Mujuru was seen watching cricket between Zimbabwe and Bangladesh on Sunday 14 August 2011, 12 hours before he died. The General was drinking [from] a glass of whisky…

Pfebve is, in fact, wrong. Contrary to his assertion, while the One Day International test was staged on Sunday 14 August, Mujuru's body was discovered in the early hours of Tuesday 16 August, and the official inquest into his death concluded that he had passed away on the night of 15 August between the hours of 8 p.m. and 3.45 a.m. Notwithstanding this discrepancy, Pfebve's post continues:

> Kasukuwere approached General Mujuru at approximately 15.30 pm on Sunday 14 August 2011 at Harare Sports Club, and soon the two started talking to each other. Supa Mandiwanzira kept a distance, he neither talked to the General, nor greeted him.
>
> General Mujuru is said to have left the Harare Sports Club at around 16 hours, after the said conversation with Saviour Kasukuwere. Both Supa Mandiwanzira and Saviour Kasukuwere left the bar immediately after General Solomon Mujuru. It is not known whether Mujuru was trailed afterwards, but what is known is that General Mujuru died 12 hours after meeting both Mandiwanzira and Kasukuwere.

However, according to the official report on Mujuru's death, he actually died about thirty hours after his 4.00 p.m. departure from the Harare Sports Club on the Sunday. Pfebve continues:

> Contrary to initial reports that the general could have been too drunk on the day of the fire, I can reveal that Solomon Mujuru was not visibly drunk at the time he left for home after meeting Kasukuwere and Mandiwanzira.

General Mujuru was pronounced dead in a mysterious fire on Monday morning of 15 August 2011, exactly 12 hours after his encounter with Kasukuwere.

This fresh information is certainly bound to ignite fresh debate on what exactly happened to General Solomon Mujuru. Is it true that the most decorated Zimbabwean soldier of our time would be killed by an inferno caused by a candle after surviving ballistic missiles and weapons of mass destruction?

According to Pfebve's narration of events, Mujuru's drinks at the Beatrice Country Club were therefore not his first that Sunday. But Pfebve appears to have been driven by a desire to 'ignite fresh debate' in order to pin the blame for Mujuru's death on Kasukuwere and Mandiwanzira, despite the thirty-hour lapse between their encounter with Mujuru at the Harare Sports Club and the time of the retired general's death the following night. Pfebve provides his theory without offering any meaningful evidence to sustain it. He even admits that he was not privy to the discussion between Mujuru and Kasukuwere. Yet through his post, Pfebve perhaps fuelled most of the speculation that Mujuru was assassinated by people linked to President Mugabe.

Logically, and contrary to Pfebve's claim, General Mujuru never faced any attacks by ballistic missiles or weapons of mass destruction during the Rhodesian Bush War. The Rhodesian Army was simply not equipped with such armaments.

It is pertinent to note that cricket officials Masunda and Chingoka – who spent a considerable amount of time with Mujuru and would therefore have also been among the last people to interact with him that Sunday, at least according to Pfebve – were never interviewed by the police or subpoenaed to testify about the events in the Captain's Pavilion on the afternoon of 14 August 2011.

Amid the flurry of speculation, an inquest into the Mujuru tragedy was appointed and forty-one witnesses were interrogated in a bid to determine the cause of the fiery blaze. When the inquest released a report that effectively put paid to the rumours, the Mujuru family and sections of the press still clung to the now established conspiracy theories. They refused to accept the verdict by the presiding magistrate Walter Chikwanha that there was no evidence of foul play.

Attorney General Johannes Tomana then instructed the police to treat Mujuru's death as a closed matter. The fact that Tomana was a somewhat discredited public official – he had been personally appointed Attorney General by President Mugabe, without the necessary consultations taking place – only reinforced the conviction of those who believed there was more to the case. Tomana stated:

I have read the record of proceedings and verdict of the presiding magistrate Mr Walter Chikwanha, and I find the verdict to be well reasoned and sound both in law and fact. I agree with the conclusion of the inquest, which finds that no foul play suspicion is sustained. In my capacity as the AG, I have accordingly recommended to the police that the docket be closed as a completed matter.

However, there remained a great deal of suspicion in some sections of the press and among much of the public, including the deceased's family and relatives, who were keen to pin a charge of murder on Mugabe. This scepticism was fuelled by several findings that came to light during the inquest's hearings: The police officer on duty was said to have been fast asleep when the farmhouse fire started. When he woke up, the officer said that he was unable to call for help because his mobile phone had run out of credit and his radio was faulty. And when the fire engine did arrive at Alamein Farm, it rather inexplicably turned out to not have any water in its tank to extinguish the blaze.

None of these details, however, amounted to evidence of murder. According to the report, 'Despite the suppositions, speculations, conjectures and suspicions by various people including the deceased's relatives, nothing concrete and no evidence at all was placed before the court to show that there was foul play in the death of the deceased.'

The magistrate also said that there was evidence from the Cuban doctor who conducted the post-mortem that the deceased did not suffer any injuries besides those caused by the fire. This differed from unsubstantiated reports of two gunshots being fired before the fire started. The Cuban doctor's credentials were questioned by lawyers representing the Mujuru family, and he faced allegations that he was not qualified or registered to practise in Zimbabwe in the first place. When he was accused of not examining the brain or the blood of the deceased during the post-mortem, he explained that there simply had been no blood or brain to examine in the charred remains left by the fire. While it was true that the doctor was not registered to practise in Zimbabwe, it was explained that he had come to the country as part of a group, in terms of an agreement between the governments of Zimbabwe and Cuba.

Magistrate Chikwanha noted:

And there is also the evidence from the lead investigator Detective Chief Superintendent Makedenge, to the effect that they carried out exhaustive investigations, but there was nothing to show that there was foul play leading to the death of the now deceased.

Experts were called to testify from ZESA [Zimbabwe Electricity Supply Authority], Fire Brigade, Police and South African forensic experts, all of them for one reason or another could not furnish the court with an explanation on how the fire started. This therefore is the basis upon which the court concludes that the cause of fire could not be determined.

The inquest's findings also dispelled the rumour that the body recovered from the farmhouse and later buried at the National Heroes' Acre was not that of General Mujuru. Chikwanha concluded:

In the final analysis the court summarizes its findings as follows: The name of the deceased is Retired General Solomon Tapfumaneyi Mujuru. This fact is clear from the factual evidence presented before the court and the DNA analysis done in South Africa. They all point to the same direction as regards to the identity of the deceased. The court also concludes that the deceased met his death between the hours of 20.20 on the night of 15 August 2011 and 03.45 on the morning of 16 August 2011.

The Mujuru family nevertheless announced a plan to petition the government to have Mujuru's remains exhumed in order for an independent examination to be performed by a doctor of their choice. The petition, however, never came to fruition.

On 23 February 2016, *NewsDay* reported that then former vice president Joice Mujuru had claimed that her late husband had been shot before his body was burnt. The article attributed this theory to an interview with Joice in the *Sunday Times*, a newspaper published in the UK.

Joice Mujuru was quoted as saying that the identity of her husband's killers would be revealed at some stage, and she pointed out that they were known to the 'people in power', meaning the top members of the Mugabe regime. When the newspaper published this allegation, it offered no fresh details or evidence; it merely narrated the original details from five years earlier and culminated in Joice Mujuru's claim of foul play.

A strange aspect of this interview is that Joice Mujuru saw it fit to make her latest accusations in a newspaper based overseas. Both *NewsDay* and its rival *Daily News* had been commendably supportive of the Mujuru family over the years by providing them with acres of front-page coverage. Yet the former vice president had taken this new dimension in the alleged shooting of her husband to the *Sunday Times* in London, leaving *NewsDay* on the spot in Harare to make do with what could be garnered from the crumbs.

Ten months later, in December 2016, Joice Mujuru sat for yet another interview with a foreign-based news organisation, the South African television station eNCA. This time, she stated as fact that President Mugabe was aware of the circumstances that led to the death of her husband. On account of that interview, the banner headline 'Mugabe knows what happened to Mujuru' graced the front page of the 8 December issue of *NewsDay*.

'He can't tell me he was not aware or he's not aware of what happened to my husband,' said Joice Mujuru, who at the time of the interview headed her own opposition party called Zimbabwe People First.

According to her argument, the idea that Mugabe could not conceivably be unaware of who allegedly killed her husband is sufficient to pass as proof of his complicity. As a journalist, I sincerely believe that even the most evil dictators are entitled to protection against unsubstantiated allegations. As a journalist, I was victimised by the government of President Mugabe. I have been wrongfully dismissed from employment. I have been wrongfully arrested by the police on the instructions of officials in the Mugabe regime. Our printing press at the *Daily News* was destroyed in January 2001, allegedly on orders from General Mujuru in a bid to please Mugabe. But as a journalist, I will do everything reasonably possible to defend Mugabe from the dissemination of unfounded allegations against him.

In June 2017, while speaking in support of Joice Mujuru, former ZANU-PF stalwart Dzikamai Mavhaire openly challenged President Mugabe to come clean on the mysterious death of the former army commander. Mavhaire, who served as the interim chair of Joice Mujuru's then recently formed National People's Party, publicly said that Mugabe could shed light on the circumstances of the general's death, if he so wished.

'You know a lot,' Mavhaire said, referring to Mugabe, 'you cannot just say you don't know. Why would this be the only thing you don't know when you seem to know everything?'

Much like Joice Mujuru's claims on the matter, this statement didn't seem to come from a position of knowledge. Rather, Mavhaire, who had fearlessly called on Mugabe to step down from power back in 1998, now appeared to be pleading with the president to confess either to killing Mujuru or to ordering his assassination.

Interestingly, the deadly fire in 2011 has a curious resemblance to an event thirty-five years earlier. In *Re-living the Second Chimurenga*, Fay Chung states that the 1976 Geneva Conference was marked by a huge fire that engulfed the Royal Hotel where the ZANU delegation was staying.

> The fire started in the room of Solomon Mujuru on the fourth floor and soon spread throughout the floor. I was on the third floor. I woke up in the middle of the night with smoke seeping into the room and when I looked out the window I saw the hotel was in flames.
>
> The question of who set the hotel on fire occupied us for some time. Within ZANU it was believed to have been caused by a Smith agent, a young overfriendly lady with revolutionary pretensions who had somehow found her way to one of the commander's rooms ... The fire had caused extensive damage to two floors of the large multi-storeyed building.

Dumisani Muleya, editor of the *Zimbabwe Independent*, conducted an interview with Mugabe which was published on 24 March 2018. In it, Mugabe spoke about Mujuru:

> Ah, he was a terrible guy. Very selfish. And a smoker. A smoker, I think this is what killed him. In Geneva, we burnt down a hotel and it was Mujuru again. Well, we managed to avoid trial, but it was his smoking that almost got us killed in a hotel. He was a careless smoker. An investigation estab-

lished that the fire started in his room. But we denied it and said no, no.

A litany of allegations that ZANU-PF had orchestrated the assassination of other key Zimbabwean politicians, both before and after independence, was enough to sustain the claim that Mujuru had been similarly eliminated. Among these accusations fall the deaths of ZANU chair Herbert Chitepo, who died in a car-bomb explosion in Lusaka, and General Josiah Tongogara, who died in a car crash in Mozambique on the eve of independence. Lieutenant General Lookout Masuku and Sydney Malunga, both formerly top-ranking ZAPU officials, as well as ZANU-PF political commissars Moven Mahachi, Robson Manyika and Border Gezi, were also alleged to have been assassinated when they died in vehicle accidents. So were ZANU-PF officials Zororo Duri and Dr Chris Ushewokunze.

The death of the journalist Willie Musarurwa, who was apparently dismissed as an editor for the *Sunday Mail* by President Mugabe for being critical of the government, was publicly attributed to food poisoning. Musarurwa had been rushed to hospital from a hotel restaurant where he had been having lunch, only to be pronounced dead on arrival. The hospital staff reported that he had died from a heart attack.

Given the constant debate that such cases have inspired, it is unsurprising that the violent death of Solomon Mujuru appeared to fit the broad pattern of suspected foul play. This perhaps gave the rumours around the tragic incident more credence than the facts themselves.

As a result, the allegation that Mujuru was assassinated has stuck with Mugabe, despite the findings of the Chikwanha inquest. But the truth of the matter might really be broader than Mugabe's accusers have wanted to argue.

As president of Zimbabwe, Mugabe created the circumstances in which the country's delivery of services collapsed. As a result of the government's maladministration, ZESA was unable to guarantee the delivery of electricity to all its subscribers. On the night of the incident, this might have forced Solomon Mujuru to light his way with a wax candle, like millions of other Zimbabweans were so often forced to do. It is also possible that the retired general – who was given to drinking rather heavily virtually every night – had fallen asleep with that candle still burning.

The disrepair of Zimbabwe's infrastructure under Mugabe could even be linked to the divisive findings during the inquest. It wasn't surprising to hear that a civil servant had been sleeping on duty. And it certainly wasn't uncommon for the condition and readiness of service equipment to have been neglected.

In these respects, President Mugabe had a large role in shaping the national circumstances that surrounded the death of Solomon Mujuru. But to claim foul play requires more than speculation. There needs to be evidence of a crime, and so far none has ever surfaced.

8

First Lady
dreams of presidency

'Even if President Mugabe dies, he will rule Zimbabwe from the grave.'   – First Lady Grace Mugabe, 2016

As Mugabe continued to age in office, his growing incapacitation became clearer to see. He lost the ability to walk unaided; he succumbed to extended bouts of sleep, even in public; and he was rumoured even to have soiled himself. A cruel photograph that revealed a catheter beneath the president's trousers went so viral on social media that I received it seven times in one day.

Apart from being embarrassing, the public display of her husband's ailments must have caused a sense of disquiet for the First Lady. While it was widely reported in the press each time he travelled to Singapore that he was seeking treatment for his failing eyesight, the appearance of the catheter suggested that he also had other, perhaps even more serious or stressful, infirmities.

The advent of social media had effectively shredded Jonathan Moyo's notorious Access to Information and Protection of Privacy Act (AIPPA). No longer could the Mugabes and fellow Zimbabwean politicians ensure that they enjoyed a controlled level of privacy. The AIPPA, which Moyo crafted and pushed through Parliament in 2001, was meant to protect politicians – even those given to nefarious activities or pursuits – from probing inquiries by the country's journalists.

When Moyo introduced the controversial bill in Parliament, the chair of the Parliamentary Legal Committee, the erudite Dr Eddison Jonas Mudadirwa Zvobgo, commented: 'I can say without equivocation that this Bill, in its original form, was the most calculated and determined assault on our liberties guaranteed by the Constitution, in the 20 years I have served as Cabinet Minister.'

As minister of information, Moyo fought many fierce battles against the media on behalf of both himself and Mugabe's government from July 2000 to 2005. He was then booted out of ZANU-PF by the president, despite his efforts.

Notwithstanding the existence of the AIPPA on the statute books, Moyo himself invaded the privacy of his fellow politicians with determination and impunity on Twitter, despite his earlier resolve to protect their reputations.

Meanwhile, Grace Mugabe tried to come to terms with the prospect of a future without her once powerful but now doddering husband. The prospects were grim. She didn't require too much encouragement from politicians such as Jonathan Moyo, Saviour Kasukuwere, Ignatius Chombo and Mugabe's nephew Patrick Zhuwao – all of whom feared the consequences of a regime change – to decide that bold steps needed to be taken. It was in those anxious circumstances that the idea likely germinated for Grace Mugabe herself to take control of Zimbabwe's future.

This led to the creation of a faction within ZANU-PF that was united in its mission to protect the First Family, most notably against the party's own 'old guard', such as Joice Mujuru and Emmerson Mnangagwa.

Those who supported Grace Mugabe were initially identified by the term Mazoe Crush, which was the name of the most popular Zimbabwean orange juice at the time. It was produced from oranges grown in the Mazowe Valley, forty kilometres north of Harare, where Grace was establishing her business and political base. In the press, the faction was dubbed the Weevils. This was after President Mugabe himself used the word at the burial of the former minister of information Nathan Magunda Shamuyarira.

'We now have weevils in our midst. ZANU-PF has weevils in its ranks,' Mugabe said in his eulogy at the National Heroes' Acre on 7 June 2014. This came at a time of heightened tension ahead of the December 2014 ZANU-PF elective congress.

Most observers were quick to regard this 'weevil' comment as a reference to Moyo, whose history as an outspoken critic of President Mugabe and ZANU-PF was well documented.

Voice of America reported on 9 June 2014 that the ZANU-PF secretary for administration Didymus Mutasa had urged Mugabe to expel the Weevils. Addressing party youths in Mutare, he suggested that they spray 'Gamatox or pesticide to destroy the Weevils'. Gamatox is the trade name of an insecticide that was widely used in Zimbabwe until it was banned. These nicknames were quickly adopted by the press, who bandied the terms around as if they were common knowledge among all Zimbabweans.

In October 2014, *NewsDay* reported that the ZANU-PF Politburo had banned the chanting of any provocative slogans. Rugare Gumbo, the party spokesperson, went on to state, 'There will no longer be "Down with Gamatox" or "Down with Weevils".' As an indication of the seriousness with which the issue of ZANU-PF factionalism was now being treated, the article claimed that President

Mugabe himself had been tasked with appointing a commission of inquiry to investigate the matter.

Grace Mugabe had significant interests to protect. Over her twenty-one-year tenure as First Lady, she had acquired real estate that was estimated to be of colossal value. She and her family are believed to own a total of fourteen sprawling commercial farming estates, obtained during the launch of the controversial agrarian revolution that started in 2000. The much-disregarded ZANU-PF Leadership Code of 1984 limits ownership of farms to only one per leader. The Mugabes also owned the Gushungo Dairy in the rich Mazowe Valley, which is about fifty kilometres north of Harare and home of Zimbabwe's famous Mazoe Orange Crush. In order to create the dairy plant in 2012, eighty newly resettled farmers were forcibly removed from farms adjacent to the Gushungo estate. The products of the dairy, which include milk, cheese, ice cream and yoghurt, trade under the name Alpha and Omega. In fact, the Omega Dairy Farm is the best known of the Mugabes' commercial farming estates and is reputed to be one of the largest dairy-farming operations in southern Africa.

In addition, Grace Mugabe owns the magnificent Amai Mugabe Junior School, also in Mazowe, on Iron Mask Farm. At its opening in January 2013, the Chinese ambassador Lin Lin disclosed that the Chinese company that had been contracted to construct the National Defence College up Mazowe Road towards Harare, and which had done the job in record time, was also responsible for building the school, with sponsorship through the Grace Mugabe Foundation.

She also constructed two palaces: Gracelands, which she sold to the late Libyan strongman Muammar Gaddafi, and the Blue

Roof, the official residence of the First Family. The construction of the latter mansion, which was completed in 2007 at an estimated cost of US$26 million, was reportedly funded by ZANU-PF as an expression of gratitude to President Mugabe for services rendered, if not to Zimbabwe as a whole then at least to the ruling party. To many in the party's upper echelons, ZANU-PF had become a veritable and exceedingly rewarding feeding trough.

The Mugabes are also believed to have made vast offshore investments in real estate. The family was reported in early 2008 to own property in Malaysia, where Grace Mugabe allegedly planned to relocate with her children in the event of her husband being dislodged from power. This move was designed to evade the stress of living in Harare without having recourse to the trappings of power, fraught as their situation was with the real threat of retribution against Mugabe.

The First Lady is also reported to have made investments in Hong Kong. They include a diamond-cutting business and a residential property. The Mugabes have offered no robust denial of these allegations.

The property was apparently acquired for their daughter, Bona, who was then studying at the University of Hong Kong, to use as a weekend retreat. However, this also gave the Mugabes the option of escaping there in the event of being ousted from power in Zimbabwe.

It was reported in 2015 that a legal dispute involving Zimbabwe had emerged over ownership of the Hong Kong property. One Hsieh Ping Sung, a South African businessperson of Taiwanese origin, had acquired the property in June 2008 for a total of HK$40 million (US$5.14 million). It had been transferred into Ping Sung's name two years later, in 2010.

This particular property was purchased at a time when Zimbabwe was at its lowest economic ebb since independence. The Mugabes reportedly alleged that the villa belonged to the Zimbabwean government, while Hsieh claimed that the house certainly belonged to the president.

For Grace Mugabe, all of this financial, political and social capital was reliant on maintaining her ageing husband's political clout.

While she was generally regarded as the leader of her faction, it was the capricious Moyo who was undoubtedly the brains behind it. Members of the group included government officials, politicians, police and intelligence officers, and businesspeople aligned to the First Lady.

Back in 2005, Moyo had confounded all when he became an independent MP for Tsholotsho after defeating both the ruling ZANU-PF and the opposition MDC in the March parliamentary elections. He was re-elected as an independent MP in 2008.

Given his history as a vitriolic critic of President Mugabe before he joined ZANU-PF and during his time in the political wilderness between 2004 and 2008, some of his fellow ZANU-PF members charged him with effectively circumventing the usual vetting processes and escaping proper scrutiny when he joined the party.

'I think Moyo used some juju because he never went through cell or branch but he just rose to the Politburo,' said ZANU-PF deputy national commissar Omega Hungwe. 'He was just catapulted to the top echelons of the party.'

In fact, it was an indication of the level of desperation on the part of the president and the First Lady that they would invest so much trust in someone as politically volatile as Moyo. Not long before, he had been quoted in the press as saying that his strategy was to destroy ZANU-PF from within. Yet this willingness for subterfuge seemed to enhance his value to the First Lady.

By many accounts, corrupt activity had shadowed Moyo since long before he joined the Mugabe government. After propelling himself to the forefront of the fight against Mugabe's desire to establish a one-party state, through articles he submitted to the *Financial Gazette* while I was the newspaper's editor, Moyo departed in mysterious circumstances, only to resurface in Nairobi, Kenya. In 1993, when he was programme director for the Ford Foundation in Nairobi, he suddenly departed again, this time under a cloud of suspicion. His departure coincided with allegations that US$88 000 had mysteriously disappeared from the organisation's coffers.

Accusations of embezzlement have since continued to dog his trail. After his relocation from Nairobi, Moyo settled in Johannesburg. He seemed to possess an uncanny capacity to move from one cushy job to another. His next appointment was on a project sponsored by the W.K. Kellogg Foundation at the University of the Witwatersrand. In January 1998, he signed a contract to work on a project called 'The Future of the African Elite'.

After his departure, the university alleged that Moyo had taken part of the R100-million research grant without informing the authorities of his pending departure. He had, meanwhile, apparently not taken the trouble to report on the future of the troubled African elite, as assigned in terms of his contract.

In October 2006, a period when Moyo was out of both office and favour with the Mugabe government, the University of the Witwatersrand and Moeletsi Mbeki, an academic and the younger brother of South Africa's then president Thabo Mbeki, each applied independently for a court injunction to have Moyo jailed if he ever stepped on South African soil again.

Around this time, I had been living in the United States, from where I maintained a mostly inimical relationship with Moyo. Through an exchange of email messages, I incurred his wrath on one particular occasion. I suggested that if he harboured any aspirations to become president of Zimbabwe himself, as I believed to be the case, then he had a major obstacle to clear. When he offered no real rebuttal to this, I went further and suggested, by way of friendly advice, that if he did in fact possess this ambition, then he must climb the highest mountain or resort to using whatever residual influence he still enjoyed at Zimbabwe Newspapers or the ZBC to embark on a national charm offensive. He would extend his profound and sincere apologies to the citizens he had angered, humiliated and deprived through his unruly conduct in seeking to silence the independent press. His actions as minister of information and broadcasting had resulted in the incarceration, destitution and outright displacement of scores of journalists, many of whom had then fled the country. That communication effectively ended my relationship with Moyo.

By 2014, Moyo had become perhaps the most unpopular politician in Zimbabwe – more unpopular, some analysts argued, than President Mugabe himself. It was in the custody of such a dubious character that Grace Mugabe entrusted her political career, with the blessings of her increasingly emasculated husband.

Grace Mugabe's bold rise to the pinnacle of power in ZANU-PF and Zimbabwean politics found momentum in her 2014 Meet the People tour, which took her to each of the country's provinces.

The programme was organised by the ZANU-PF secretary for the commissariat Saviour Kasukuwere, and it received logistical support from Moyo. Ten new vehicles purchased for the ministry's Information and Media Panel of Inquiry (IMPI), of which I was the chair, were commandeered from the programme and diverted to the First Lady's nationwide tour, with a huge quantity of diesel being fraudulently taken to fuel them. From October to December 2014, a total of 2 000 litres a month were diverted to Grace Mugabe's tour. Meanwhile, even though US$43 000 had been allocated in the budget for the printing of the IMPI report, I was forced to resort to fund-raising US$25 000 in order to cover the printing costs. The project had run out of funds.

To further influence public perception of the First Lady, Moyo made calculated use of social media, where he blazed a trail on Twitter, much to Mugabe's initial annoyance. The president regularly castigated ZANU-PF officials who waged intra-party squabbles on social media platforms.

Moyo, however, routinely ignored the president's outbursts and occasionally tweeted even as Mugabe denounced his tweets. In due course, Mugabe seemed to realise that Grace was a direct beneficiary of Moyo's ardent Twitter campaign and gradually became less vocal in his condemnation of it. This was especially so as his wife developed a stronger presence and louder voice of her own.

At a rally in the town of Marondera in Mashonaland East Province, Grace Mugabe took the opportunity to publicly denounce Ray Kaukonde, who was the former ZANU-PF Mashonaland East chairperson and provincial governor. In a sustained diatribe, she announced that he had once been loyal to President Mugabe but had since fallen out of presidential favour. This had happened when he was accused of supporting a rival faction of the party, alleg-edly led by then vice president Mujuru.

Kaukonde, who remained unfazed, became an instant hero and a darling of television viewers who saw him defy the First Lady when she ordered him to rise and stand before her. Other ZANU-PF officials had jumped to their feet when ordered to do so by Grace Mugabe. Press photographers had captured telling images of Mash-onaland Central provincial minister Martin Dinha and then home affairs minister (and one of Zimbabwe's richest cabinet ministers) Ignatius Chombo both genuflecting before the First Lady, to the amazement of onlookers. Didymus Mutasa, the former minister for presidential affairs, had also kowtowed before the First Lady when he arrived to pay his condolences after the death of the presi-dent's sister earlier that year. Given that it is not common practice among either the Shona or the Ndebele people of Zimbabwe for a man to genuflect before a woman, regardless of her status, this must have been a highly uncomfortable experience for both the president and the minister. The incident also provided an indication of how the president's power was in decline, while the First Lady's was rising.

With regard to Kaukonde, some media reports suggested that the spat between Grace Mugabe and him was the result of a business deal gone sour, rather than factional combat within ZANU-PF. By all accounts, the conflict didn't involve President Mugabe himself – only the First Lady.

Kaukonde was powerful as a shareholder in and director of Innscor Africa Limited, which operates the Spar retail franchise in Zimbabwe. Grace Mugabe reportedly blamed Kaukonde after she failed to reach an agreement to operate a supermarket under the Innscor franchise in Harare. An online news service published a detailed account of the conflict between the First Lady and Kaukonde, which led to her directing the president to send him packing.

'Grace Mugabe could not fulfil the conditions for operating a Spar supermarket,' the article reported. 'She tried to arm-twist Kaukonde to allow her to open the shop without conforming to the global Spar standards but he refused. That is the real source of her beef with him.'

The report claimed that Grace Mugabe had wanted to take over an existing TM Supermarket somewhere in the Harare city centre. She had been informed of changes and improvements that needed to be made on the building in order to have it conform with the standards of the Spar brand, but she had allegedly refused to do this. Instead, she had attempted to negotiate a deal with Kaukonde to bypass the required specifications. Kaukonde had turned her down. That is when she apparently decided to label him a political rival and an ally of Vice President Mujuru, leading to his expulsion from ZANU-PF.

Kaukonde had reportedly been forced to flee Zimbabwe soon afterwards, following a raid on his home by CIO agents. Managing to evade them, Kaukonde fled across the border into South Africa, abandoning his Mercedes-Benz in the border town of Beitbridge.

As an interesting aside, back in 1989, at the height of the Willow-gate scandal, it was rumoured that First Lady Sally Mugabe had also sourced vehicles from Willowvale Motors and had allegedly used Kaukonde to collect them. One of the ministers implicated in the scandal, Dr Callistus Dingiswayo Ndlovu, handed over to the San-dura Commission a piece of paper that apparently revealed the identity of someone who had not been named by *The Chronicle*. There was much speculation that the name scribbled on that piece of paper was Sally Mugabe's.

Although our own investigation at *The Chronicle* did not uncover her name in the context of looting from Willowvale, some of the ministers involved accused me of having covered up for her. They seemingly convinced the president that unless I was quickly removed from the newspaper, I would embarrass him by exposing his wife's alleged corruption.

Apart from this orchestrated attack on Kaukonde in 2014, the main target of Grace Mugabe's nationwide tour was Vice President Mujuru. Over the course of several months, Joice Mujuru's political career and her long-standing association with ZANU-PF were effectively trashed. There wasn't an iota of doubt in any politically savvy Zimbabwean's mind as to what the game plan actually was: Grace Mugabe wanted to be recognised as a viable candidate to ascend the throne.

Just in case an O-level certificate from Kriste Mambo Secondary School near Rusape and another certificate from one of the nondescript but burgeoning secretarial training colleges in Harare were viewed askance by the political establishment, her husband, in his capacity as chancellor of the University of Zimbabwe and all other state universities, conferred upon her a PhD in sociology in 2014. Unsurprisingly, the First Lady's doctoral thesis was never deposited in the university archives, despite this being required. This took place two months before she hit the ground as a serious candidate for presidential office, and only two months after she had registered for the university programme. Amid the turmoil created in the Zimbabwean academic community, with some commenting that it had caused irreparable harm to the university's reputation, all hell soon broke loose.

The ears of faithful ZANU-PF members were assailed at the Meet the People rallies with wild claims that Joice Mujuru was plotting against President Mugabe. She was accused of using juju in her bid to achieve her presidential ambitions. The polarised newspapers, reporters and over-quoted political analysts, some of them self-styled, savoured every moment of the unfolding drama. One *Sunday Mail* issue carried a lengthy article detailing Joice Mujuru's sexual exploits in Mozambique during the war, before she had married Solomon Mujuru. Such was the vicious extent of her vilification. Meanwhile, newspaper readers were fed a pot-pourri of fact and opinion, which often left them totally confused as to what exactly was happening in Zimbabwean politics.

'The youths have alerted me about someone who is spearheading factionalism in this province and I told Baba [President Mugabe] to "baby-dump" that person. I told him that if he does not dump the person, we will do it ourselves,' Grace Mugabe told a rally in October 2014 in the Mashonaland Central town of Bindura, Mujuru's stronghold. It was not clear whether the First Lady's 'we' was the royal 'we' or whether it signified the instant conscription of the youths of Bindura as accomplices in the bid to depose the vice president from office.

'Her attack on Mujuru is something we have never seen before and a declaration of war,' the *Zimbabwe Independent*, one of the more reliable purveyors of news and information in Harare, quoted a ZANU-PF official in Mashonaland Central as saying. 'We have never heard her or the President even attacking Tsvangirai like that. She has gone too far.

'She also made it clear that she was targeting Mujuru and said she would take matters into her own hands if the President does not "baby-dump" her. We are wondering where she is getting that power from. Is she saying she is now in charge of the party and country and can now do as she pleases?'

It was clear that the First Lady had the blessing of her ailing husband. 'Mrs Mugabe wields a shadow power in her husband's presidency,' said Nkosana Moyo, who once served in the Mugabe cabinet as a technocrat. 'Although she is not elected she behaves as though she were elected herself.'

Another politician to openly challenge Mugabe as the factional rifts within ZANU-PF widened was the war-veteran leader Jabulani Sibanda. Before he became chair of the Zimbabwe National Liberation War Veterans Association, Sibanda was a former ZIPRA combatant.

Towards the end of October 2014, Sibanda vowed that he would continue to boycott Grace Mugabe's rallies until she stopped her public attacks on then vice president Joice Mujuru. Sibanda said that he was ready to defend this position and warned that genuine war veterans would resist attempts by Grace to stage a coup.

'I am not going to allow any coup either in the boardroom or in the bedroom,' said Sibanda in an interview with *NewsDay*. 'If you want to find me guilty of not attending the First Lady's rallies, I plead guilty on that one and I won't attend unless the programme changes.'

'I can't attend a function where they say, "*Pamberi neMazowe Crush, pasi neGamatox.*" That slogan is unknown in ZANU-PF,' Sibanda declared. 'That slogan is divisive and counter-revolutionary. You can't belong to a group that insults a vice president of the country.'

This was a direct challenge to Grace Mugabe and, by extension, the president. Translated into English, the slogan means 'Forward with Mazoe Crush and down with Gamatox'.

In a bid to silence Sibanda, he was expelled from leadership of the ZNLWVA. He was also arrested and prosecuted for allegedly contravening a controversial insult law through his 'bedroom coup' utterances. Sibanda, however, walked out of court a free man after the state dropped the charge that he had insulted the president.

At the time of his acquittal, Sibanda had been on remand for more than two years. During this period, the state had failed to prosecute him, resulting in his case being repeatedly postponed.

Apart from allegedly accusing President Mugabe and the First Lady of plotting a 'bedroom coup', Sibanda was reported to have stated that 'power is not sexually transmitted'.

More seriously, the state also accused Sibanda of threatening to mobilise war veterans to march on the State House. The source of this charge was a meeting held on 27 October 2014 at Herbert Mine in the Mutasa District of Manicaland.

State prosecutors claimed that the war veterans' leader had delivered a long speech there, during which he said that the Mugabes were plotting to remove Vice President Mujuru from office and to replace her with the First Lady.

As Vice President Mujuru faced this public humiliation, Grace Mugabe sampled her first taste of political victory. By arrangement, Oppah Muchinguri, the secretary of the powerful ZANU-PF Women's League, stood down from the coveted position and was replaced by none other than the First Lady. Her nomination as head of the Women's League received the resounding approval of the delegates by acclamation on 6 December 2014. In her new position, she also became a member of the ZANU-PF Politburo.

Two days later, Joice Mujuru was fired, along with eight cabinet ministers, all of whom were linked to her. The nine officials were accused of orchestrating a plot to topple Mugabe from power. Among those dismissed were presidential affairs minister Didymus Noel Edwin Mutasa, who was also party secretary for administration; labour minister Nicholas Tasunungurwa Goche; indigenisation minister Francis Dunstan Chenaimoyo Nhema; higher and tertiary education minister Olivia Nyembezi Muchena; information communication technology minister Webster Kotiwani Shamu, who was also the ZANU-PF political commissar; and Mashonaland East provincial affairs minister Simbaneuta Mudarikwa.

But the expelled vice president countered this charge by claiming that she was being victimised for exposing infiltrators who were allegedly conspiring to destroy ZANU-PF, which by then had ruled the country for thirty-four years. 'I have become the fly in the web of lies whose final objective is the destruction of ZANU-PF and what it stands for and ultimately the present government,' Mujuru said in a statement.

Mujuru was accused of plotting not only to overthrow Mugabe but also to have him assassinated. In the eyes of ordinary Zimbabweans, this was clearly a fabrication. Mujuru was never arrested or prosecuted on the serious charges levelled against her in public. But, by the time of the ZANU-PF elective congress that same month, she had become a veritable outcast within the party.

Her long-time rival Emmerson Mnangagwa assumed the position of vice president on 10 December. Even though Mujuru dismissed the wild claims against her as ridiculous, she was nevertheless expelled from ZANU-PF on 3 April 2015, alongside several senior politicians who were identified with her faction. These included Dzikamai Mavhaire, of Masvingo Province; Rugare Gumbo, the official spokesperson of the party; Ray Kaukonde, ZANU-PF's Mashonaland East chairperson and governor of the province; and Didymus Mutasa, the party's secretary for administration, who had been particularly close and loyal to the president.

Yet all of this unfolded in public without the president's intervention. He observed in silence as many of his former allies were disgraced and ejected from office on spurious grounds. It was quite apparent that the main beneficiary of these manoeuvres was Grace Mugabe, not the president himself.

The general impression was that President Mugabe had become something of a prisoner in the State House. Reinforcing this notion were his increasing displays of frailty, such as succumbing to bouts of slumber during meetings, missing his step as he walked in front of anxious or amused audiences, and even once relentlessly ploughing through the wrong speech.

Some commentators, though, have portrayed the Mugabes' relationship as being more symbiotic. In their view, Mugabe benefited from his wife's public performances, while she exploited these opportunities to practise at being president.

But the consequences of such reckless leadership are very real, and the Mugabes' removal of their political rivals would prove to be strong evidence of this.

9

The rise and fall of the Crocodile

'If you see people coming after you even in football, it means you are the one in possession of the ball.'
– Vice President Emmerson Mnangagwa, 2016

After Emmerson Mnangagwa became vice president, the dynamics within ZANU-PF changed and intensified, and its factions took on different names. Grace Mugabe's group was known as Generation 40, or G40, referring to the fact that the majority of Zimbabweans were under forty years old. Grace herself was still in her forties at the time, and was seen to represent the younger generation.

The Mnangagwa group became known as Lacoste, named after the Lacoste clothing company, established by the French tennis star René Lacoste and his business partner André Gillier. One of the company's most famous products is its golf shirt, recognisable by its famous green crocodile logo. As a tennis player, René Lacoste earned the nickname the Crocodile because of his tenacity on the court. In Zimbabwe, decades later, Mnangagwa earned the nick-name Garwe ('Crocodile' in the indigenous Shona language) for his tenacity on the political landscape. In due course, the faction under Mnangagwa unofficially adopted the logo of the French clothing company, thus placing its formidable stamp on Zimbabwean politics.

The more confident that Grace Mugabe grew that political victory was within her reach, the more aggressive and abusive she became. As her public tirades continued with impunity, her husband sat behind her listening dutifully. On most occasions, he appeared to be dozing off.

In discussions about his level of engagement, people often argued that even if he wasn't awake for her speeches, he would still have been aware of their content, having approved them after consultation with her. This debate was more fierce than usual in the case of the First Lady's excoriation of George Charamba, her husband's official spokesperson and the government's ingenious chief spin doctor.

Charamba was the press secretary in the Office of the President, as well as permanent secretary in the Ministry of Information, Media and Broadcasting Services. In his position as the president's spokesperson, Charamba carried immense authority and influence. The stature of his office was even further enhanced through shrewd manipulations by Charamba himself. Previous incumbents of the office, such as Godfrey Paradzai Chanetsa (who was treated by Sally Mugabe as her own son), Andrew Mutandwa and Lindiwe Sadza, had never exuded so much clout, even though Sadza was the daughter of Dr Davidson Sadza, who was chair of the Zimbabwe Mass Media Trust and Zimbabwe Newspapers (1980) Ltd. Dr Sadza was a friend of Mugabe's from their student days at Fort Hare University in the Eastern Cape.

Born in the Buhera District of Manicaland in 1963, Charamba is the holder of an English degree from the University of Zimbabwe. He was awarded the British Foreign and Commonwealth Office Chevening Scholarship, which he used to study for a master's degree in media studies at Cardiff University in Wales. Armed with such an impressive array of credentials, Charamba arrogated to himself the status of owner and controller of Zimbabwe's media, while trampling on the rights and freedoms of journalists, publishers and politicians, many of whom came to live in mortal fear of him.

He buttressed his position by constantly churning out a venomous column for *The Herald* every Saturday. The Nathaniel Manheru column, a commentary of phenomenal length and pompousness, was used initially by Jonathan Moyo as minister of information and later by Charamba as a tool for attacking the perceived enemies of ZANU-PF, Mugabe, the government and, so some said, Charamba himself.

On 28 January 2016, he was interviewed on the ZiFM Stereo radio station of information communication technology and cyber security minister Supa Mandiwanzira, the only station ever registered in the name of an individual Zimbabwean at the time. The presidential spokesperson, who was believed to be aligned with Vice President Mnangagwa's Lacoste faction, said the following in apparent reference to Jonathan Moyo:

> There are many sinister minds that speak in the name of the President, who are in fact secessionists and it won't be long before the headlines give you the story. Some have been meeting Nicodemusly [secretly] with the People First, but they are still in ZANU-PF ... Here are little men with absolutely no iota of history behind them thinking they can one day emerge as leaders of this country with their little minds thinking baldness is age, it isn't ... The Constitution of Zimbabwe is as clear as daylight. One tragedy of those little fellas, and I call them little fellas, they confuse media skills with

social skills. They think you can scale up a political ladder by tweeting, who think when you manipulate one or two headlines, you have a social base for launching your stupid ambitions, they will come to grief, get it from me.

Stung by Charamba's castigation of her key political allies, Grace Mugabe took her husband's spokesperson, eloquence and all, head-on. At a public rally, she accused him of failing to reprimand sections of the media for 'attacking National Commissar, Saviour Kasukuwere, and Higher Education Minister, Jonathan Moyo, day-in and day-out'.

She said that media outlets were being used to malign Kasukuwere and Moyo, with allegations being made that Kasukuwere wanted to remove President Mugabe from office. 'Every day we read about Kasukuwere. If it's not him, then it's Professor Moyo. People have gone to the extent of coming up with non-existent corruption cases,' she claimed to the utter amazement of many.

Summoning Charamba to where she was standing, Grace Mugabe said: 'George, I have known you for a while, way before you were appointed to your current position and before I was First Lady ... So, I want to reprimand you as your mother. You are junior to Ministers. I notice there are some people who get favourable coverage and others not. Why?'

While Grace Mugabe publicly defended Kasukuwere and Moyo, a staggering nine of the ten provinces had just expressed a vote of no confidence in Kasukuwere.

The First Lady further surprised her audience when she referred to herself as Mugabe's third assistant. A party insider was reported as saying that it was this kind of political immaturity that would work against Grace Mugabe if ever she wanted to rise to the top of ZANU-PF.

Included in this behaviour was her growing tendency to rant at public meetings, which raised genuine concerns about the state of her mind. Her husband, the president, would passively listen whenever she did so. One rumour that started to circulate with increasing frequency was that Irene Marufu, Grace's mother, had long become a person of doubtful mental stability. Some less charitable commentators suggested that her daughter was now following in the footsteps of her mother.

Nevertheless, by the time that Kudzanai Chipanga had launched the party's Million Man March on 25 May 2016, the First Lady was well positioned to make her ambitions a reality.

Of all her G40 allies, Chipanga was one of her most devoted. Despite being a man of limited literacy, he was an MP for Makoni West and the ZANU-PF secretary for youth affairs. His plan was a carbon copy of the Million Man March held in October 1995 in Washington D.C., organised by the controversial religious leader Louis Farrakhan as a huge gathering of African American men.

Addressing the hundreds of thousands of marchers, Grace Mugabe said that the ZANU-PF Women's League was fully behind the visionary leadership of her husband, who would be difficult to replace as president of Zimbabwe. She went on to state:

> As the Women's League, we are going to support you. Some want you to be life President, but we say you are irreplaceable to the Presidency.
>
> We will appoint you President even in your grave at the National Heroes' Acre because you are our unifier. You are

faithful before the Lord. Before you were even born, God knew you.

You were set apart because God did not want you to mix and be contaminated by evil.

Amid these outlandish remarks, the G40 faction used this event to begin its onslaught on Vice President Mnangagwa. This took the form of an unprovoked attack by Mandiitawepi Chimene, which shocked even ardent ZANU-PF stalwarts. While Chimene was the MP for Makoni South constituency and minister of state for Manicaland provincial affairs, her performance in both roles was largely steeped in mediocrity, and she was better known as one of Grace Mugabe's more sycophantic legmen in the ZANU-PF Women's League.

Chimene's behaviour was guided by one unflinching principle: always please the First Lady. After Chimene fled from Zimbabwe following the downfall of the Mugabe regime, the finance minister Patrick Anthony Chinamasa described her as having been 'an arrogant leader, who exposed her poor leadership skills through continuously harassing and threatening civil servants'.

When Morgan Tsvangirai went public with the news in June 2016 that he was suffering from colon cancer, Chimene reportedly claimed that the MDC-T leader was paying the price for having wished death on President Mugabe. In addition to celebrating Tsvangirai's illness, Chimene even resorted to such immaturity as attacking his looks: 'If you look at his face that is what is in his brains. He is not appealing. He is ugly. You should not vote for him, because he is a loser.'

This was the calibre of some of the politicians who were propping up the Mugabe regime. Sarah Mahoka, who publicly revealed that she was unable to read or write despite being a legislator, is another example. Such politicians were given leeway in order to castigate and humiliate those in the ZANU-PF leadership whom the First Family perceived as political opponents.

In her attack on Mnangagwa, Chimene publicly accused him of clandestinely fronting a plot to usurp Mugabe's powers and of running parallel government structures.

The vice president felt obliged to respond. Arguing that he was being targeted by his detractors in the ruling party, Mnangagwa said that his opponents were trying to drive a wedge between him and Mugabe because, as vice president, he had become a powerful figure. He denied that he was a 'secessionist', as his accusers were claiming, and vowed that he would not be distracted: 'Do I look like I care? I am not moved by those false allegations. They can continue barking, barking and barking, while I continue working for ZANU-PF and my President.'

Chimene called on President Mugabe to expel Mnangagwa from both the party and government – 'the Joice Mujuru way,' she said, according to *NewsDay*.

It is pertinent to note that while Mugabe's deputies – Mnangagwa and Joice Mujuru before him – were constantly disparaged by his surrogates, such as Grace Mugabe and Chimene, the president rarely directly attacked them himself. His silence, however, in failing to raise his voice in their defence was palpable.

There was much speculation that the president's silence was, in fact, a tactical strategy and that Grace Mugabe's constant disputes were not without his approval. This was interpreted as an indication of how politically weakened he had become.

'If you cannot [fire Mnangagwa now],' Chimene protested, 'then we propose that you call for an extraordinary congress. We will help you to expel him.' She described Mnangagwa as a problem animal that deserved to be culled. On his part, Mnangagwa maintained his cool during this highly charged meeting, which was organised by a small pro-Mugabe faction of war veterans led by Chimene and hordes of ZANU-PF supporters, who were reportedly bussed in to show solidarity with the Mugabes.

According to Mnangagwa, this all had to do with his political power. 'If you see people coming after you even in football,' he said, 'it means you are the one in possession of the ball.'

Through this showdown, the intra-party battle lines were laid bare.

Inspired by what the G40 faction viewed as the success of the Million Man March, Chipanga and his handlers, Moyo and Kasukuwere, went back to the drawing board, this time to devise plans for the forthcoming Presidential Youth Interface rallies. This would be Grace Mugabe's final push to secure the ZANU-PF vice presidency at the party's elective congress in December 2017.

As before, a central tactic for G40 was eliminating the First Lady's rival candidates for presidential office. The prime targets, of course, were Vice President Mnangagwa and his Lacoste faction.

With the president, the First Lady and the various G40 luminaries in tow, Chipanga dashed from province to province in what was designed as a massive show of force, intended to inspire fear not only in the ranks of G40's factional rivals but also in the parties constituting the opposition MDC Alliance.

Some observers dismissed the rallies as nothing more than an opportunity for Chipanga to ingratiate himself with the First Family through a level of personal support that came across as fawning. He had even taken to calling the president 'Angel Gabriel', to the general consternation of Zimbabweans, many of whom are devout Christians. At a June 2017 rally in Marondera, Mashonaland East, Chipanga made the following pronouncement: 'Truly speaking, in heaven there is God and here on earth there is an angel called Robert Gabriel Mugabe. You are representing God here on earth.'

Otherwise, at every available opportunity, and clearly drunk on borrowed power, Chipanga chanted *'Munhu wese kuna Amai'*, which is Shona for 'Every person should rally behind the Mother of the Nation.' Yet, for all his fervour, it seemed as though the only person to take Chipanga seriously was the First Lady. Meanwhile, Chipanga was beginning to show conspicuous signs of living well.

Later that month, the president and his entourage travelled to Masvingo Province for the third leg of the nationwide rallies. There, Mugabe revealed plans for a populist and vote-buying scheme to transform loyal youths into instant landlords by providing them with 20 000 free residential stands.

'We are very thankful to President Mugabe who saw it fit for youths in Masvingo Province to be proud landlords by giving us residential stands for free,' said the ZANU-PF Masvingo provincial youth chairperson.

In parting, Mugabe urged the youths to give their support to the rallies.

By this stage, the feud between the G40 and Lacoste factions was nearing its peak intensity. The incident that brought their conflict to a head was the alleged consumption of poisoned ice cream by Vice President Mnangagwa.

This happened in the Matabeleland South capital of Gwanda on the sixth leg of the Presidential Youth Interface rallies, on 12 August 2017. Mnangagwa had suddenly fallen seriously ill and started vomiting, resulting in his being airlifted to the Midlands town of Gweru, then further north to Harare, and finally south again, all the way to Johannesburg.

After initial suggestions that Mnangagwa had been poisoned with ice cream from the Mugabes' Gushungo Dairy, this event degenerated into a volley of humiliating attacks on the vice president. He exposed himself to further derision when he denied that he had ever been poisoned with Gushungo ice cream.

Although President Mugabe was increasingly frail at ninety-three years old, it was still considered treasonous for anyone, Mnangagwa especially, to entertain the aspiration of succeeding him as head of state. Garwe, or the Crocodile, as Mnangagwa was popularly known, paid heavily as a consequence.

With tensions already higher than usual, the very next day nevertheless brought with it a new controversy. On 13 August, Grace Mugabe shocked the world when she physically attacked Gabriella Engels, a twenty-year-old South African model in Johannesburg. As details of this embarrassing incident emerged, it turned out that the First Lady had descended fiercely on Engels, who had been partying with Grace's convivial two sons Robert Jr and Chatunga Bellarmine in the plush hotel where they were staying.

The assault left Engels with a serious injury on her forehead, caused by the plug of an extension cord that Grace Mugabe had used to beat her. Engels immediately took the matter to the police, while circulating pictures of her wound on social media. According to Engels, the First Lady's bodyguards had simply watched as she was assaulted. 'She split my head open in three places with an extension cord and used the plug to hit me,' explained Engels.

A major diplomatic row was averted only when Grace Mugabe was accorded diplomatic immunity – which she was not legally entitled to – much to the chagrin of South African human rights activists and lawyers who were preparing to take her on in court. Ducking out of the media, she piggybacked on the presidential flight back to Harare, where she quietly licked her wounds and tried to put the incident behind her. To counter this negative publicity, Chipanga quickly organised a solidarity march for Grace Mugabe on 30 August.

Yet despite these efforts to control the Mugabes' public image, a new controversy soon arrived, this time involving Grace Mugabe's first-born son, Russell. On 17 September, he did the unthinkable and imported two Rolls-Royce Phantom limousines, estimated to have cost US$280 000 each, before even factoring in import duty and freight charges.

'The move has angered many poor families who battle to put food on the table in a country battling rampant unemployment and worsening poverty,' reported South African journalist Peta Thornycroft in the *Pretoria News*.

Tendai Laxton Biti, an opposition politician who served as minister of finance from 2009 to 2013, offered several acerbic remarks. 'This family are toxic parasites,' he said. 'What is Russell going to do with his Rolls-Royces on the potholed roads around Harare?'

While expressing his incredulity, Biti poignantly pointed out that Russell, like Grace Mugabe's other sons, had failed to pass a single school-leaving examination. 'Nearly 80 percent of Zimbabweans are living in extreme poverty,' Biti explained, 'yet we have this insane first family – the Mobutu Sese Sekos of our time – squandering taxpayers' money on houses for Grace in South Africa and now Rolls-Royces for her son.'

The limousines' delivery was apparently cause for the president's wayward stepson to celebrate in his customary style. He was heard to boast that his next import, an Aston Martin Super Sport, was scheduled to arrive in Harare soon.

By early November 2017, the mood in Zimbabwe had started to shift. And despite increasingly passionate efforts, the wheels were beginning to come off the seemingly unstoppable G40 juggernaut. Chipanga, Moyo and Kasukuwere had underestimated the political landscape while overestimating their own abilities to persuade the people of Zimbabwe to accept the First Lady as her husband's successor.

In the latter period of Mugabe's reign, the lustre of his presidency had diminished. The number of people celebrating independence had shrunk, and attendance at Independence Day events had become limited to hard-core ZANU-PF loyalists and those who were enticed by entertainment provided by top-notch musicians and soccer teams. Even many of the party faithful had become disillusioned with Mugabe's lacklustre or outright unsatisfactory performance. This was exacerbated by the grievous decline in the economy, which saw the demise of the Zimbabwean currency and its replacement with the controversial bond note in 2016, resulting in anxious depositors scrambling to withdraw their US dollars from the country's banks. The political turmoil on top of this, stemming from rampant corruption and the mismanagement of state affairs by Mugabe and his acolytes, further drove home the severity of the situation.

A point of no return in the deteriorating relationship between

President Mugabe and the people of Zimbabwe was soon to be passed. Surprisingly, the moment came at the ninth edition of the Presidential Youth Interface rallies, held at White City Stadium in Bulawayo on 4 November 2017.

During this event, Grace Mugabe seized the opportunity to discount her critics and bolster her position among ZANU-PF's more loyal supporters. She pronounced:

I am the First Lady, and I will stand for the truth. If you don't want to hear what I am saying, that is your problem. But I will tell you what is there.

The only man who is ruling this country is President Mugabe. Period. We don't want factionalism here. We don't want it. Jonathan Moyo was appointed by the President and you must know that.

Some of you were paid to boo me. Go ahead and boo. I don't care. I am the First Lady and I will stand for the truth.

Yes, let me tell you something. You can bring soldiers with guns to shoot me and I will still say the same thing. I will never stop saying it. We don't want our party to be divided. There is factionalism here. Down with those responsible.

Yes, we are going to Congress and the person we are going to support is the leader of ZANU-PF, the President, Mugabe, my husband. I know they sent you to boo me when I speak. Come on, boo. Go ahead and do it. I don't care.

The level of booing immediately rose to an uproar, a deafening crescendo. It was the first public and unmitigated display of such resistance to the Mugabes. Completely undeterred, however, the

First Lady ploughed on with her tirade. She proceeded to exonerate the ZANU-PF national political commissar, Saviour Kasukuwere, of any wrongdoing. Meanwhile, demonstrations had recently been staged across the country to denounce Kasukuwere and demand his removal from office.

With the party's elective congress now only a month away, Vice President Mnangagwa persisted in being Grace Mugabe's biggest obstacle. To her advantage, despite her husband's political decline, he still held the power of the presidency.

Yet even so, it was clear to all that dismissing Mnangagwa would not be as simple as it had been with Joice Mujuru. Mugabe's allies who controlled the party's disciplinary apparatus were met with resistance by those loyal to the vice president, including leaders of the ZNLWVA who had been expelled from the party.

Nonetheless, on 6 November 2017, President Mugabe invited a political crisis by doing the absolutely unthinkable: he summarily dismissed Mnangagwa. Among the reasons he gave for the firing were disloyalty and conduct inconsistent with the performance of the vice president's official duties.

Two days later, Mnangagwa fled from Zimbabwe, later claiming that there had been 'incessant threats' against him and his family. This was his second emergency trip to South Africa, the first being just three months earlier for his medical treatment in Johannesburg, amid speculation that his G40 rivals were responsible for poisoning him.

When Joice Mujuru had been dismissed from office in December 2014, the task of making the announcement was assigned to the chief secretary in the Office of the President and Cabinet, Dr Misheck Jameson Mpande Sibanda, which was procedural. On the occasion of Mnangagwa's expulsion – which happened in very similar circumstances – the announcement was relegated to the Ministry of Information, Media and Broadcasting Services.

Simon Khaya-Moyo, the recently appointed minister there, read a press statement on Mnangagwa's removal. Flanked by George Charamba, his permanent secretary, and Anyway Mutambudzi, the director of media services, the new minister perfunctorily performed what was clearly an unpleasant task:

> In accordance with the Constitution of Zimbabwe Amendment Number 20 Act of 2013, Section 329, 6th Schedule, Paragraph 14, Sub-paragraph 2, His Excellency the President Cde R.G. Mugabe has exercised his powers to relieve Honourable Vice President E.D. Mnangagwa, of his position as Vice President of the Republic of Zimbabwe with immediate effect.
>
> It had become evident that his conduct in the discharge of his duties had become inconsistent with his official responsibilities. The Vice President has consistently and persistently exhibited traits of disloyalty, disrespect, deceitfulness and unreliability.
>
> He has also demonstrated little probity in the execution of his duties.

The statement was signed by Khaya-Moyo. The nation was stunned.

But even as the G40 faction celebrated its victory, a military response to Mnangagwa's dismissal was already being fine-tuned. In nine short days, the entire country would wake up to the news of the Mugabe regime being irrevocably overthrown.

10

The night of the long knives

'We are only targeting criminals around [Mugabe] who are committing crimes that are causing social and economic suffering in the country in order to bring them to justice.'
— Major General Sibusiso Moyo, 2017

The military operation on 14 November 2017 that forced an end to Mugabe's controversial rule was masterminded by General Constantino Guveya Chiwenga, the commander of the ZDF. Despite President Mugabe's orders for the military not to engage in politics, General Chiwenga had made the decision to intervene.

The peaceful manoeuvre, which was executed with surgical precision, was code-named Operation Restore Legacy. As events unfolded, not only Zimbabwe but the whole world was taken by surprise. However, instead of resolving the confrontation between the two warring factions in ZANU-PF, the overthrowing of the government escalated the conflict to an entirely new level of intra-party hostility.

While the generals were at pains to emphasise that they had not staged a military coup d'état, the reality was that the government of President Mugabe had been forcibly dislodged after thirty-seven years in power. By securing the First Family inside their Blue Roof mansion, General Chiwenga had effectively seized control of Zimbabwe, both militarily and politically. Apart from those in the ranks of the G40 faction, the operation had managed to avoid antagonising too many people. Both in Zimbabwe and in the international community, the majority of people had long supported an end to Mugabe's dictatorship, and they were now quietly accepting the sudden developments taking place and the peaceful transfer of power being promoted.

Early in the morning of 15 November, television viewers in Zimbabwe were greeted by the appearance on their screens of ZDF spokesperson Major General Sibusiso Moyo, clad in full military gear. The state broadcaster, the ZBC, had also been taken over by the military during the night.

Major General Moyo, who had been a fighter with ZIPRA during the war of liberation and who, as it was soon revealed, was a close ally of General Chiwenga, was stern in his demeanour as he explained to anxious Zimbabweans and the world at large the nature of the events taking place. The full military statement, as delivered that morning, is worthy of quoting in full:

Good morning Zimbabwe
Fellow Zimbabweans. Following the address we made on 13 November 2017, which we believe our main broadcaster, Zimbabwe Broadcasting Corporation, and *The Herald* were directed not to publicise, the situation in our country has moved to another level.
Firstly we wish to assure our nation that His Excellency, the President of the Republic of Zimbabwe and Commander-in-Chief of the Zimbabwe Defence Forces, Comrade R.G. Mugabe and his family, are safe and sound and their security is guaranteed.

We are only targeting criminals around him who are committing crimes that are causing social and economic suffering in the country in order to bring them to justice.

As soon as we have accomplished our mission, we expect that the situation will return to normalcy.

To the civil servants, as you are aware, there is a plan by the same individuals to influence the current purging which is taking place in the political sphere. To the civil service, we are against that act of injustice and we intend to protect every one of you against that.

To the judiciary, the measures underway are intended to ensure that as an independent arm of the state you are able to exercise your independent authority without fear of being obstructed as has been the case with this group of individuals.

To our Members of Parliament, your legislative role is of paramount importance to peace and stability in this country, and it is our desire that a dispensation is created that allows you to serve your respective political constituencies according to democratic tenets.

To the generality of the people of Zimbabwe, we urge you to remain calm and limit unnecessary movement. However, we encourage those who are employed and those with essential business in the city to continue their normal activities as usual. Our wish is that you will enjoy your rights and freedoms and that we return our country to a dispensation that allows for investment, development and prosperity that we all fought for and for which many of our citizens paid the supreme sacrifice.

To political parties, we urge you to discourage your members from engaging in violent behaviour. To the youth, we call upon you to realise that the future of this country is yours. Do not be enticed with the dirty coins of silver, be disciplined and remain committed to the efforts and values of this great nation.

To all churches and religious organisations in Zimbabwe, we call upon your congregations to pray for our country and preach the gospel of love, peace, unity and development. To both our people and the world beyond our borders, we wish to make this abundantly clear that this is not a military take-over of government. What the Zimbabwe Defence Forces [are] doing is to pacify a degenerating political, social and economic situation in our country which, if not addressed, may result in violent conflict.

We call upon all the war veterans to play a positive role in ensuring peace, stability and unity in the country. To members of the Zimbabwe Defence Forces, all leave is cancelled and you are all to return to your barracks with immediate effect.

To the other security forces, we urge you to cooperate for the good of our country. Let it be clear that we intend to address the human security threats in our country. Therefore any provocation will be met with an appropriate response.

And to the media, we urge you to report fairly and responsibly.

We thank you.

When Moyo said that 'the situation in our country has moved to another level', most of the millions of people listening had no idea of the developments that had already taken place overnight. It was clear, though, that the proceedings under way were not confined to a single event. They were initiated by a series of events over a period of time, and they involved a number of players on Zimbabwe's political landscape. Among these was General Chiwenga himself.

Back in 1973, Chiwenga was a teenager of seventeen years at Mount St Mary's Mission, a Catholic institution in the Hwedza District of Mashonaland East Province, near the town of Marandellas (a corruption of the name Marondera by colonial settlers at the turn of the nineteenth century; the town's name quickly reverted to Marondera after independence). Accompanied by some classmates – including Perence Bigboy Samson Shiri, who became commander of the Air Force of Zimbabwe after independence, and another who became Brigadier General Etherton Shungu of the Mechanised Brigade of the ZNA – Chiwenga absconded from the school, which was well known for its close links with ZANLA.

They undertook an epic journey on foot, heading across Manicaland Province and finally the country's eastern border to enter Mozambique. Many other schoolchildren at the time were doing exactly the same: abandoning their education in Rhodesia and crossing into Mozambique or Zambia to train as ZANLA or ZIPRA guerrillas. In Chiwenga's case, his training took place in both Mozambique and Tanzania.

Having adopted the *nom de guerre* Dominic Chinenge, he was deployed into war zones in the eastern and southern regions of Rhodesia, where ZANLA was engaging the Rhodesian forces in the Bush War. As Chinenge, he was initially appointed provincial commander of the ZANLA guerrilla army's Gaza sector in the southern Masvingo province. Not long after, in 1978, he was promoted to ZANLA's high command as deputy political commissar under Josiah Tongogara.

When the two guerrilla armies were integrated with the former Rhodesian Army to form the new ZNA after independence, he was given charge of 1 Brigade in Bulawayo as a brigadier. Following his promotion to the rank of major general, he reverted to his original name, Constantino Chiwenga.

After independence, he received further training, this time under British military instructors. However, he allegedly failed the Basic Officers' Course at the Zimbabwe Staff College.

In 1994, on the establishment of the ZDF, Chiwenga was promoted to the rank of lieutenant general and was appointed commander of the ZNA. On the retirement of General Vitalis Zvinavashe in 2004, Chiwenga rose to become the commander of the ZDF.

After serving in this role for a decade, Chiwenga was thrust into the forefront of Zimbabwean national politics owing to the factional infighting that followed the death of the former ZNA commander Solomon Mujuru in 2011.

While President Mugabe urged the military not to engage in politics, especially those of ZANU-PF, insisting that the military must remain disciplined and separate, General Chiwenga openly defied him in August 2016, causing the relationship between the president and the military to turn frosty.

The general attitude on the part of the military leadership was that they were ZANU-PF stockholders; therefore, they felt legitimately entitled to be involved in party politics. This sentiment was captured in Major General Moyo's televised statement on 15 November 2017.

In a long interview that was serialised in the *Sunday Mail*, Chiwenga made several unequivocal and rather ominous declarations, the target audience of which could only have been the leadership of ZANU-PF and, in particular, President Mugabe.

'We are apolitical to the extent that we leave you to do what you like,' Chiwenga said, 'but the moment you threaten the sovereignty of the country, then you threaten that very Constitution. Please don't expect us to sit and watch. We are there to protect the people and that's what we are saying and will do.'

Chiwenga's remarks were an indication that although President Mugabe was commander-in-chief of the ZDF, he had lost control of the military and was being openly defied by his own generals.

Chiwenga also appeared to issue a thinly veiled attack on Jonathan Moyo and Mandiitawepi Chimene, both G40 linchpins, who were fighting for Grace Mugabe to take over the presidency instead of Vice President Mnangagwa. Despite their efforts, however, Mnangagwa maintained the support and backing of both the powerful war veterans and the military.

Ostensibly, the military was motivated by a determination to ensure that the candidate they backed to succeed Mugabe had the potential to safeguard the military's interests and influence. Accordingly, members of the G40 faction were viewed as a threat.

The war veterans issued a communiqué in which they claimed that Mugabe was the brains behind G40 and the one fomenting disunity in ZANU-PF. They claimed that it had always been Mugabe's strategy to create factions within the party in order to preserve his leadership position. In particular, the war veterans were at loggerheads with Mugabe over his reluctance to openly name a successor and his heavy-handed approach to dealing with those who discussed the issue.

The security chiefs promised to investigate and expose the

authors of the communiqué, but not much came of their investigations, especially since the war veterans enjoyed the support of the military establishment.

When President Mugabe went ahead with firing Mnangagwa on 6 November 2017, he thereby threatened the military's agenda. At this time, General Chiwenga was out of the country on an official visit to Beijing, China. While there, Chiwenga was reported to have met senior Chinese military officials, including generals Chang Wanquan and Li Zuocheng. This led to speculation that Chiwenga's visit to Zimbabwe's only remaining friend among the Big Powers was directly linked to the plot to overthrow Mugabe in Harare. There were further rumours that Chiwenga had, in fact, sought Beijing's tacit approval for a possible move against Mugabe.

The Chinese Foreign Ministry immediately dismissed such speculation, saying that Chiwenga's visit was nothing more than a 'normal military exchange'. Meanwhile, the Chinese Embassy in Pretoria, South Africa, furiously dismissed the reports of Chinese collusion in the developments in Harare as 'self-contradictory, full of logical fallacies and filled with evil intentions'.

While still in Beijing, Chiwenga received intelligence that Mugabe was not simply lying low while waiting to be deposed by the military. He had in fact issued an instruction for General Chiwenga to be arrested upon his arrival back at Harare International Airport. Information has subsequently surfaced that on the general's return to Zimbabwe, soldiers loyal to the ZDF commander had disguised themselves as baggage handlers and overpowered the police detail that had been deployed to ambush him and were lying in wait at the airport. Only then was the way cleared for Chiwenga's passage through the airport on Sunday 12 November 2017. The head of the

Zimbabwe Republican Police, Commissioner General Augustine Chihuri, and director general of the CIO, Happyton Bonyongwe, were later said to have been supporting the president.

Within a day of his arrival back in Harare, Chiwenga sprang into action and issued a terse statement on 13 November. The following are some of its highlights:

> It is pertinent to restate that the Zimbabwe Defence Forces remain the major stockholder in respect to the gains of the liberation struggle and when these are threatened we are obliged to take corrective measures.

> What is obtaining in the revolutionary Party is a direct result of the machinations of counter-revolutionaries who have infiltrated the Party and whose agenda is to destroy it from within.

> It is saddening to see our revolution being hijacked by agents of our erstwhile enemies who are now at the brink of returning our country to foreign domination against which so many of our people perished.

> It is our strong and deeply considered position that if drastic action is not taken immediately, our beloved country Zimbabwe is definitely headed to becoming a neo-colony again. The current purging and cleansing process in ZANU-PF which so far is targeting mostly members associated with our liberation history is a serious cause for concern to us in the Defence Forces.

> As a result of squabbling within the ranks of ZANU-PF, there has been no meaningful development in the country for the past five years.
>
> We must remind those behind the current treacherous she-nanigans that when it comes to matters of protecting our revolution, the military will not hesitate to step in.

Few Zimbabweans had forgotten Jonathan Moyo's comment that, after challenging Mugabe from without, he had adopted a strategy of seeking to destroy ZANU-PF from within.

The statement by Chiwenga was hard-hitting. It was tantamount to a threat to Mugabe and Moyo of a possible military takeover. Both the ZBC and *The Herald*, the flagship of the government-controlled Zimbabwe Newspapers stable, totally ignored the statement. There is little doubt that this was owing to instructions from George Charamba at the Ministry of Information, especially in the aftermath of his being severely reprimanded by the First Lady. The failure or refusal by the media to publish what was clearly a major story must have been the final straw for the military.

While the nation pondered exactly what Chiwenga meant by his references to 'corrective measures', 'drastic action' and 'the military ... step[ping] in', Kudzanai Chipanga rashly waded into the turmoil and delivered a televised statement of his own the very next day. 'Defending the revolution and our leader and president is an ideal we live for and if need be, it is a principle we are prepared to die for,' he said.

It was quite evident, however, that Chipanga was out of touch with reality. Late on 14 November, reports started to circulate on social media that soldiers in tanks and armoured personnel carriers were heading south along Lomagundi Road towards the capital city. They were deployed from Inkomo Barracks, about forty kilometres north of Harare, which is the base of the ZNA's Mechanised Brigade.

Two mechanised infantry battalions and one armoured regiment comprise the brigade. The armoured regiment has three squadrons of armoured cars and one squadron of tanks. The armoured cars are Cascavels of Brazilian origin, which were purchased by the ZNA soon after independence. The tanks are an assortment of Russian, Chinese and North Korean T-54 and T-55 main battle tanks. These are what rolled into Harare during the night.

Several roads in the capital city were immediately blocked off. These included the road leading to the Blue Roof, the Mugabes' private residence, and one leading to the ZBC at Pockets Hill in Highlands, which was sealed at the security checkpoint. It was reported that on the arrival of the military, some members of the national broadcaster staff were roughed up by the soldiers.

In the early hours of Wednesday 15 November, the military spokesperson, Major General Moyo, then appeared on ZBC TV to allay any fears that the military had conducted a coup d'état, as was widely feared.

It later transpired that between sunset on Tuesday and dawn on Wednesday, when Major General Moyo appeared live on television, the Blue Roof and the residences of several ZANU-PF politicians and government ministers had been overrun by the military, with those ministers being arrested or detained. Among them were finance minister Ignatius Chombo and the First Lady's loyal running dog Kudzanai Chipanga. The latter was allegedly beaten up and then forced to publicly apologise in front of television cameras for having read the statement that denounced the military's top brass. He was then brought to court on charges of attempting to destabilise and cause disaffection among the security forces. Patrick Zhuwao, Mugabe's nephew, was known to be overseas at the time of the takeover and was safely beyond the military's dragnet. But Jonathan Moyo and Saviour Kasukuwere had somehow managed to disappear; only rumours on social media claimed knowledge of their whereabouts.

11

The long march that shaped history

'Whom the gods would destroy they first make mad.'
– Henry Wadsworth Longfellow, 'The Masque of Pandora', 1875

On 18 November 2017, a fortnight after the acrimonious youth rally in Bulawayo, the anti-Mugabe momentum began to spread across the country. The people organised themselves into a mass uprising that consisted of different races, religious persuasions, ages and even political affiliations. Travelling in busloads from all corners of the country, they had responded to exhortations by the ZNLWVA, which was acting with the overt backing of the ZDF, opposition political parties and various civil society organisations. Several ZANU-PF vehicles were also observed in the melee. After all, it was ZANU-PF supporters who had challenged the Mugabes at White City Stadium in the first place.

A mammoth crowd, estimated at half a million people, descended on the famous Zimbabwe Grounds in Highfield in a mass demon-stration of national unity. There they were addressed by leaders of the country's various political parties, ranging from President Mugabe's own ZANU-PF to the MDC Alliance of Morgan Tsvangirai. It was a carnival-like atmosphere of peaceful celebration as had never been witnessed in Zimbabwe. Then, bearing strongly worded placards that denounced the Mugabes and extolled the newly discovered virtues of the military, the crowd set off on the long eighteen-kilometre march to the State House in Harare. One of the common slogans being held aloft was 'Zimbabwe Army: The Voice of the People'.

As the march poured into the city, which was already clogged with other demonstrators who had been converging there since morning, its progress was hampered by the bulk of the masses in the Avenues area between the city centre and the State House. By late afternoon, the route bounded by Josiah Tongogara Avenue to the north and 7th Street to the east couldn't absorb any more marchers, regardless of their determination to reach the State House and add their voice to the protest against the Mugabes.

By around 4 p.m., the march had created a massive gridlock, trapping hundreds of thousands in the Avenues area and making further movement – whether towards the State House or back into the city – a real challenge. My vehicle was trapped for more than an hour in Josiah Chinamano Avenue at its intersection with Mazowe Street, near the Avenues Clinic, where protesters had simply parked their vehicles in the road. Many of the car boots were left open to help blast the music being played as people danced to the tune of the moment, 'Kutonga Kwaro' by Jah Prayzah. It was a song dedicated to Emmerson Mnangagwa, who was then on his way back from his brief exile in Johannesburg.

As the Mugabes watched the televised coverage from within the Blue Roof, they must have been astounded by the spectacle of blacks, whites, Indians and coloureds joining hands with the soldiers who had descended from their massive tanks to sing, dance and celebrate in the streets. They must have observed with dread that their fierce hold on the people of Zimbabwe was gone.

On the day of the march, political parties graciously discouraged their supporters from donning any party regalia. This was done to help reinforce a spirit of national togetherness. Social media also played a significant role in motivating and uniting Zimbabweans of all races. In the past, members of the white, Indian and coloured communities had not usually graced such political events or gatherings with their presence.

This made the march a political event that was entirely without precedent, even though the reasons to protest had already been there for several decades, going back to the emergence of the opposition crusade, spearheaded by Tsvangirai's MDC, in September 1999.

Since then, Zimbabweans had endured a steady decline in the performance of the national economy, accompanied by the government's failure to ensure the provision of basic goods and services. In parallel to this, they were forced to watch as politicians indulged in brazen corruption, which manifested in the construction of enormous mansions around the northern and north-eastern suburbs of Harare. Such construction projects were initially contracted by the captains of industry and top executives in the mining sector, which was understandable. However, government ministers and military chiefs, as well as the new kids on the block, the so-called 'men of god', also moved into these exclusive areas, which was not always comprehensible.

In Harare, investigations by the *Zimbabwe Independent* revealed that Grace Mugabe had siphoned off millions of dollars during her husband's umpteen trips overseas. 'On one occasion this year, for instance, his wife took about US$3.5 million during a foreign trip,' a senior Treasury official revealed to the newspaper. 'There is also another example – the money used to buy their mansion in Sandhurst, Sandton, Johannesburg in South Africa came from public funds through local banks.' It was further alleged that Grace Mugabe had once demanded of Patrick Chinamasa, the minister of finance, that he should source funds for her to purchase cars and that he had obliged.

As for President Mugabe himself, a US diplomatic cable back in 2001, which was subsequently released by WikiLeaks, suggested that Mugabe had about US$1.75 billion worth of personal assets, most of them invested outside Zimbabwe. According to the cable, although reliable information was difficult to access, there 'were rumours that his assets include everything from secret accounts in Switzerland, the Channel Islands and the Bahamas, to a castle in Scotland'. This means that the actual details of Mugabe's much-discussed foreign assets remain in the realm of anecdote. However, there has never been a robust denial of this leaked information.

The president is reported to have purchased a US$5.2 million mansion in Hong Kong in 2013 and also to own Hamilton Palace in Sussex, England, which was estimated to be worth about US$40 million. Again, no meaningful denials have been issued by Mugabe.

When the army tanks rolled into Harare on 14 November, Chinese contractors had been in the process of hacking away the side of a hill in the northern precincts of the city in order to create space for the construction of yet another Mugabe mansion. This one had been for their daughter, Bona. As she said of her father in the Dali Tambo interview: 'You have always been there for me … financially. You are always taking care of us. I have everything I need.'

The Mugabe children had attended fine universities in Dubai, Hong Kong, Singapore and South Africa. Incredibly, Bona's first board appointment after graduation was on the Censorship Board of Zimbabwe. Meanwhile, her husband, Simba Chikore, was appointed chief operating officer of Air Zimbabwe at about the same time. In contrast, fellow graduates from the University of Zimbabwe and the country's other mushrooming institutions of higher learning were often eking out a living by vending cellphone airtime or tomatoes on the streets of Harare.

Having trashed and lost faith in the efficacy of the country's once excellent health-delivery system, the president now constantly flew to Singapore to receive treatment for himself in first-class medical facilities. This typically amounted to US$4 million per trip. To add insult to national injury, when Bona was ready to deliver her first baby, the Mugabes' hospital of choice was again in Singapore, far away from the clinics of Harare. Some Zimbabwean women still deliver their babies at home without vital prenatal care, especially in the rural areas, where they don't always have easy access to medical facilities.

The yawning chasm between the Mugabes and the majority of the country's citizens had steadily become too wide to bridge. Then the president and his spouse had orchestrated the humiliating dismissal of Vice President Mnangagwa. In these circumstances, it is no surprise that the people of Zimbabwe had needed little motivation to turn out in the hundreds of thousands to protest against the Mugabe regime on 18 November.

The following day, buoyed by the resounding success of the march and bowing to pressure from the powerful war veterans, ZANU-PF convened an emergency meeting of its Central Committee. By then, except for dyed-in-the-wool G40 protagonists, virtually all others – from card-carrying ordinary members to officials in the upper echelons of the party – were portraying themselves as supporters or sympathisers of the Lacoste faction.

As a consequence of that meeting, the Central Committee removed Grace Mugabe as head of the ZANU-PF Women's League and barred her from the party for life. Phelekezela Mphoko, the lacklustre second vice president, was also summarily dismissed. Mphoko had served for a troubled three years, the highlight of which was when he incurred the public's wrath by remaining firmly ensconced in a five-star hotel suite for more than a year with his wife, children and grandchildren, all at taxpayers' expense. Other prominent G40 figures, such as Saviour Kasukuwere, Jonathan Moyo, Patrick Zhuwao, Ignatius Chombo, Walter Mzembi, Makhosini Hlongwane, Samuel Undenge and Sarah Mahoka, were also expelled with immediate effect.

The anger against Kasukuwere was compounded by the fact that he epitomised the brazen corruption that had become a characteristic feature of ZANU-PF. Like the Mugabes, he had obtained multiple farms since 2000. These are reported to include part of Pimento Farm in Mashonaland Central, owned by Oliver Newton; South Bamboo Creek, which was jointly owned by N. Richardson and R. Morkel in Shamva; and Cornucopia Farm Orchard, whose owner was Interfresh Limited. Kasukuwere also took possession of the 500-hectare Harmony Farm in Mazowe, followed by Bretton Farm, Auchenburg Farm and Bourne Farm. The gem in his real-estate portfolio, however, is said to be an enormous mansion in the northern outskirts of Harare, containing some fifty rooms. There was nothing in these acquisitions by Kasukuwere that even remotely suggested a desire to satisfy a legitimate need for land or to redress colonial imbalances in land distribution.

In addition to his vast estates, he is said to have also acquired several commercial companies. Until 2005, he was the executive director of Comoil. He was also the owner of Migdale Holdings Limited and Allen Wack & Shepherd, a long-established transport company, and is reported to be a significant shareholder in Inter-fresh Limited.

This massive accumulation of property, wealth and influence is truly remarkable for such a young man. In an environment where one's climb up the political ladder was usually linked to his or her liberation-war credentials or pedigree, the ascent of Saviour Kas-ukuwere, who was only nine years old when Zimbabwe attained independence in 1980, is truly phenomenal.

On Sunday 19 November 2017, the Central Committee at ZANU-PF headquarters turned its attention to resolving the matter of President Mugabe. The decision was made not only to immediately dismiss him as president and first secretary of the party, but also to give him a maximum of twenty-four hours to resign as president of Zimbabwe and commander-in-chief of the ZDF.

The atmosphere that followed this meeting was surreal. The Central Committee members danced with reckless abandon that afternoon, especially the ZNLWVA's chairperson Chris Mutsvangwa, who had previously been expelled from ZANU-PF and had been in the forefront of organising the mass revolt against the Mugabes. Even Michael Chakanaka Bimha, Grace Mugabe's own cousin, took part in the celebrations. Less sure of foot on the dance floor were characters such as Sydney Sekeramayi, a prominent fence-sitter in ZANU-PF's factional disputes, even when the G40 faction had tried to propel him as a presidential candidate to succeed Mugabe.

What Morgan Tsvangirai's MDC had failed to accomplish in eighteen years of political struggle, the military had achieved in just ten days under the leadership of General Chiwenga. At her recent rally, the First Lady had taunted for soldiers to come with their guns and shoot her. In an unprecedented show of military might, the soldiers of the ZDF had given their response. While experts argued over the legality and constitutionality of Operation Restore Legacy, one fact was clear: the military had brought the Mugabe regime to a commanding halt.

12

The fall of an aged dictator

'No matter how good a dancer you are, you must always know when to leave the stage.' — Kenyan proverb

In the early evening of 19 November 2017, the first stages of President Mugabe's highly anticipated resignation were somehow both drama-filled and anticlimactic.

On the day of his final reckoning, this widely feared and supposedly untouchable leader had not cut much of an impressive or fearsome figure. He was led into a prepared room at the State House, almost like a sheep to the slaughter. There, he slumped rather pathetically into the chair reserved for him at the solitary table.

Dwarfed on either side by the imposing figures of General Chiwenga to his right and Father Fidelis Mukonori, who had become a constant companion and adviser to the president, to his left, Mugabe simply focused on the papers before him. He hardly dared to raise his head. Gone was the customary confidence, bordering on defiance, that had become both his practice and his trademark whenever he addressed the nation, sometimes for several hours on end.

Arranged on the table, waiting to spread his words around the world, were two ancient-looking microphones, one of them from the notoriously compliant state broadcaster, which was now under military control. Otherwise, there was only a single ZBC television camera. The rest of the media, comprising a burgeoning contingent of local and foreign journalists who had descended on Harare like vultures to document the dramatic turn of events, were prohibited from entering the State House.

As a result, the event's coverage was rather spartan despite the historic weight of the occasion: Mugabe was expected to resign as president of the country, commander-in-chief of the ZDF, president and first secretary of ZANU-PF, and chancellor of Zimbabwe's state universities.

The atmosphere was tense. But as Mugabe sat there before the television camera, it struck me as incomprehensible that Zimbabweans had ever been petrified of him at all. After so many decades, he looked like any other harmless old man – vulnerable and perhaps a little frightened. In reality, though, it was the men lined up to Mugabe's right who had instilled such fear among the people on his behalf. Now those generals had turned on Mugabe.

Next to General Chiwenga sat Zimbabwe's security chiefs. They included Dr Augustine Chihuri, commissioner general of the Zimbabwe Republic Police; Lieutenant General Philip Valerio Sibanda, commander of the ZNA; Air Marshal Perence Shiri, commander of the Air Force of Zimbabwe; and Commissioner General Paradzai Zimondi of the Zimbabwe Prisons and Correctional Services. Standing at the far right and striking a rather dissonant note in civilian garb was the acting director general of the CIO, Aaron Daniel Tonde Nhepera.

On the other side, by Father Mukonori, were Dr Misheck Sibanda, the long-serving chief secretary in the Office of the President and Cabinet, and George Charamba, the permanent secretary in the Ministry of Information, Media and Broadcasting Services, who served as the official spokesperson for President Mugabe. It was the same Charamba who had only recently been castigated in public by Grace Mugabe during her rally in Bindura.

Members of the public who were anxiously watching on television were expecting a succinct statement by the president that he was finally resigning from office. His years in power had been tumultuous and excruciatingly painful for the majority of Zimbabwe's ordinary citizens. More than three decades of dire economic decline had resulted in a dwindling availability of everyday goods, not to mention serious cash-liquidity crises in banks and other financial institutions. They were years characterised by the ostracisation of Zimbabwe from the international community.

As Mugabe prepared to read, there was a moment of embarrassment as he fumbled with the sheets of paper in his hands and some detached themselves, only to be quickly rescued by General Chiwenga, who leaned forward to retrieve them from the floor. Quite astonishingly, rather than returning them to the president, he handed the papers to Dr Chihuri, who accepted and held onto them. The reason for this odd exchange has remained a mystery.

But the often voluble ZNLWVA later claimed that this small act of clumsiness was no accident. There were reports that the fallen papers retrieved by Chiwenga had been the president's letter of resignation. It was thus alleged that Mugabe had used the opportunity to discard his speech in order to avoid delivering it.

When he was sacked as leader of the ZANU-PF party the previous day, a Saturday, Mugabe had been given until noon on Monday to resign as head of state. If he did not, he would face the risk of being impeached when Parliament, then on recess, reconvened on Tuesday 21 November.

With this deadline in place, ZANU-PF published a draft impeachment motion. The draft stated that Mugabe had become a 'source of instability' and had shown disrespect for the rule of law. It also placed the blame for Zimbabwe's economic nosedive over the past fifteen years entirely on Mugabe's shoulders.

While the nation expected him to steel himself and reward them with his instant resignation that Sunday evening, Mugabe proceeded, much to the consternation and chagrin of those watching him, to read a statement that was tantamount to a routine State of the Nation Address. The event struck most as a colossal disappointment. In his final televised speech to the public, Mugabe had not even offered significant concessions to a nation of anxious citizens. Among the most disappointed, however, were the army generals who had orchestrated the military takeover during that week.

All that millions of people had hoped to hear was a simple declaration: 'I hereby tender my resignation from the position of president of the Republic of Zimbabwe.' Instead, there Mugabe sat, glum and nervous, a mere shadow of his reputation, with his eyes fixed on the papers now neatly arranged for him to read.

The idea that his speech had been swapped is certainly not implausible. It was suggested by those who appeared to be in the know that there had been a last-minute realisation that the president, in terms of Section 96 (1) of Zimbabwe's Constitution, could only resign by tendering a letter to the Speaker of the House of Assembly. Simply having him read a statement to the nation would not be legally or constitutionally binding.

In fact, Chiwenga had hinted as much when he revealed that negotiations had gone well between the generals and the president, and that Mnangagwa was on his way back to Harare from his brief exile in South Africa. Chiwenga had correctly pointed out that it was not the responsibility of the military to announce the resignation of the president to the nation. This might explain the withdrawal of Mugabe's papers and their concealment by Chihuri, which left the president looking uncharacteristically unsure of himself.

During his twenty-minute speech, Mugabe merely acknowledged that Zimbabwe was a country beset with problems. And to the utter astonishment of all who were watching, he vowed to soldier on. 'The era of victimisation and arbitrary decisions must end,' he said.

Unbelievably, Mugabe went on to declare that he would preside over the forthcoming ZANU-PF congress, then a few weeks away in December, despite the fact that the party's Central Committee had dismissed him as president and first secretary just a few hours earlier.

'I will preside over its processes, which must not be prepossessed by any acts calculated to undermine it or to compromise the outcomes in the eyes of the public,' Mugabe maintained. He did not explain how he intended to oversee the congress if he was no longer the leader of the party.

Since it was patently clear that Mugabe had no intention of resigning from office that Sunday night, the nation's focus became riveted on the noon deadline the following day. Yet it came and went, and the president had still not provided his resignation. The House of Assembly immediately started to galvanise for a final onslaught on Mugabe through impeachment.

Mugabe's first encounter with trouble on Tuesday 21 November was a general boycott of that morning's cabinet meeting. Only three ministers, Michael Bimha, Joseph Mtakwese Made and Edgar Mbwembwe; chief secretary to the president and cabinet, Dr Misheck

Sibanda; and Attorney General Prince Machaya showed up. Mugabe had convened that particular meeting at the State House instead of in the usual cabinet room at Munhumutapa Building.

That same morning, upon his arrival back in Harare, Mnan-gagwa issued his first statement. He implored the president to take heed of what he called the insatiable desire for change by the country's population. 'The people of Zimbabwe have spoken with one voice,' said Mnangagwa, 'and it is my appeal to President Mugabe that he should take heed of this clarion call and resign forthwith so that the country can move forward and preserve his legacy.'

Later in the afternoon, lawmakers from both Houses of Parlia-ment, reinvigorated by the events of the past week, assembled in the Harare International Conference Centre, which was large enough to accommodate the joint sitting. They proceeded to go through the formalities of pushing forward the impeachment motion. Among Mugabe's alleged flaws that were cited were his falling asleep in public during meetings and permitting his spouse, Grace Mugabe, to 'usurp presidential powers'.

The motion was tabled by Senator Monica Mutsvangwa of ZANU-PF and seconded by James Maridadi of the MDC-T, the main opposition party.

But Mugabe, who remained a cunning politician to the end, scuttled the whole process. Amid proceedings, an usher hesitantly walked into the hall and approached the Speaker, Jacob Mudenda. While handing over a letter, the usher mumbled a short message. Although his voice was too soft for onlookers to hear, the mean-ing of the exchange was obvious. His Excellency, President Robert Mugabe, had finally resigned.

The timing of the letter's arrival effectively denied the honourable members their first and only opportunity to humiliate Mugabe through impeachment, as they had been busy planning to do.

The members erupted in celebration as Speaker Mudenda went through the process – perhaps a mere formality in the circumstances – of reading out the president's resignation letter. What follows is a transcript of that letter as it was read to the joint sitting of the senate and the House of Assembly:

> In terms of the provisions of Section 96, Sub-Section 1, of the Constitution of Zimbabwe, Amendment Number 20, 2013.
>
> Following my verbal communication with the Speaker of the National Assembly, Advocate Jacob Mudenda at 13:53 hours, 21st November, 2017 intimating my intention to resign as the President of the Republic of Zimbabwe, I, Robert Gabriel Mugabe, in terms of Section 96, Sub-Section 1 of the Constitution of Zimbabwe, hereby formally tender my resignation as the President of the Republic of Zimbabwe with immediate effect.
>
> My decision to resign is voluntary on my part and arises from my concern for the welfare of the people of Zimbabwe and my desire to ensure a smooth, peaceful and non-violent transfer of power that underpins national security, peace and stability.
>
> Kindly give public notice of my resignation as soon as possible as required by Section 96, Sub-Section 1 of the Constitution of Zimbabwe.
>
> Yours faithfully,
> Robert Gabriel Mugabe,
> President of the Republic of Zimbabwe

On that sombre note, Mugabe's reign – characterised by over three decades of political intimidation, violence, gross abuses of human rights, deprivation through shortages of basic commodities and the inadequate provision of essential services – drew to a close. As Mudenda finished reading Mugabe's letter, the response was deafening. The members of the two Houses rose as one in instant celebration, with dancing and cheering.

As word spread from the conference centre like wildfire, mostly through various social media platforms such as WhatsApp, Facebook and Twitter, which had become the most reliable sources for the latest information in Zimbabwe, the citizens of Harare once more poured out onto the streets in an extraordinary demonstration of merriment and triumph.

Beyond the streets of the capital city, the breaking news was similarly welcomed by the rest of the country. Meanwhile, many major foreign powers – particularly those in the West – were cautiously optimistic about the developments under way. Both the UK and the US appealed for Zimbabwe to follow a peaceful transition to democracy.

Although Mugabe had started out as a hero of the liberation struggle against racist white minority rule, he had not reached the end of his reign with that same reputation. Instead, he stepped away as the man who had reduced his country to a husk of its former self, from a shining diamond and breadbasket in 1980 to a country whose people wallowed in poverty, misery and fear.

Three days after Mugabe's departure, Emmerson Mnangagwa, former vice president and Mugabe's long-time ally until earlier that month, was sworn in on 24 November as the new president of the Republic of Zimbabwe and commander-in-chief of the ZDF. The well-attended inauguration ceremony was conducted at the National Sports Stadium, under the watchful eyes of the nation's liberation-war heroes whose remains are interred across Bulawayo Road at the National Heroes' Acre.

Despite the optimism of the moment as Mnangagwa assumed the presidency, the mounting national expectations could easily have led to a crisis. The challenges ahead of the new president and his government were truly gargantuan. Giving further shape to the pressure, this remarkable political turnaround was occurring after years of hostility between Zimbabwe and the major Western nations.

The UK minister for Africa, Rory Stewart, who was in Harare to witness Mnangagwa's inauguration, expressed confidence that Zimbabwe could be developed to greatness, with a new administration now in place. Stewart shared these hopeful sentiments upon his return to London. He described the former British colony as one of the wealthiest countries in Africa. 'It has incredible human resources potential, a very educated population and fantastic natural resources, but it is a country which has suffered terribly,' he said.

Opposition leader Morgan Tsvangirai told the BBC that he hoped that Zimbabwe had embarked on a 'new trajectory' that would include free and fair elections. As for Mugabe, Tsvangirai said that he should be allowed to 'go and rest for his last days'. Tsvangirai's own enthusiasm for the unfolding events would have been tempered by his personal circumstances. He was afflicted with colon cancer and was constantly travelling to South Africa to seek medical attention. As a result, his position as MDC-T president during this time was insecure, an issue compounded by the constant bickering for leadership among his three vice presidents: Thokozani Khupe, Nelson Chamisa and Elias Mudzuri.

The British prime minister Theresa May also issued a statement. She said that Mugabe's resignation as president of Zimbabwe provided the country with an opportunity to 'forge a new path, free of the oppression that characterized his rule ... As Zimbabwe's oldest friend, we will do all we can to support this, working with our international and regional partners to help the country achieve the brighter future it so deserves.'

The US Embassy in Harare shared similar sentiments. 'We congratulate all Zimbabweans, who raised their voices and stated peacefully and clearly that the time for change was overdue,' its statement said. 'Zimbabwe has an opportunity to set itself on a new path. Through that process, the United States urges unwavering respect for the rule of law and for established democratic practices. Whatever short-term arrangements the government may establish, the path forward must lead to free, fair and inclusive elections.'

Essentially, the strategy that Mnangagwa needed to adopt was that of seeking to reverse the more glaring of Mugabe's detrimental policies. Taking measures to ensure free and fair elections would be a great starting point. Following that, an appropriate rectification of the harmful aspects of the land-reform programme would restore the viability of Zimbabwe's once-prosperous commercial-farming sector. Compensation for the farmers who were dispossessed, not necessarily for the land but for structural improvements, would similarly be a valuable step. So too would be a serious address of the Gukura-hundi campaign, which has remained a sore point for Zimbabweans since the 1980s, especially in the western regions of the country.

Another contentious issue for the new president to tackle is the rampant corruption that has been widely blamed for collapsing the economy. Mindful of this, Mnangagwa immediately declared a three-month amnesty period for the return of any stolen funds, especially those stashed abroad.

An anti-corruption dragnet was also spread out by Mnangagwa's new government in the months of December 2017 and January 2018. As a result, the police arrested a number of government ministers, all of them belonging to ZANU-PF's G40 faction, on charges that ranged from corruption and fraud to abuse of office. Those arrested included Walter Mzembi, formerly the minister of tourism and very briefly of foreign affairs; Makhosini Hlongwane, formerly the minister of sport, arts and recreation; Samuel Undenge, the minister of energy and power development; and Joseph Made, the minister of agriculture, mechanisation and irrigation development.

A search of storage facilities at Made's farm in the Rusape area in December 2017 unearthed a strange stockpile of goods that were in short supply in Zimbabwe. They included bags of a 2006-vintage fertiliser and, quite bizarrely, a number of serviceable wheelchairs. At the time, many desperate disabled citizens had been routinely featured on ZBC TV, frantically appealing for a wheelchair.

A budget delivered by Patrick Chinamasa, the minister of finance and economic planning, who had been axed by Mugabe and reinstated by Mnangagwa, sought to increase investor confidence by promising a 'new economic order'. This entailed the government reducing its spending and taking it easy on the indigenisation laws that force companies to cede 51 per cent of their shareholdings to black Zimbabweans. In the past, the recipients had most often been the politicians themselves and their political cronies.

An additional challenge for Mnangagwa was creating a new cabinet. Although there were strong expectations that he would include some members of the opposition, he selected mostly loyalists from the Lacoste faction of ZANU-PF. He also did not forget to reward the army generals who had paved his own way to the State House. General Chiwenga became one of the two vice presidents, while Air Marshal Shiri, commander of the Air Force of Zimbabwe, was appointed minister of lands, agriculture and rural resettlement. Major General Sibusiso Moyo, who had made the public announcement of the military takeover on 15 November, became Zimbabwe's new minister of foreign affairs and international cooperation.

In a symbolic move, the King George VI Barracks was then renamed the Josiah Magama Tongogara Barracks on 6 December, in honour of the liberation-war icon.

Meanwhile, the phrases 'new dispensation', 'ease of doing business', 'stable investment destination' and 'Zimbabwe now open for business' became part of the lingo at all the ensuing business conferences, from those in Harare all the way to the World Economic Forum in Davos, Switzerland. There, Emmerson Mnangagwa – the man from Africa who had recently done the unthinkable and overthrown the Mugabe regime – was one of the most prominent guests. Alex Magaisa, the doyen of Zimbabwean political analysts, commented:

His was a late invitation to Davos, in recognition of the vastly changed circumstances of Zimbabwe following Mugabe's dramatic exit. He has his own slot on a busy Davos programme filled with political heavyweights, where he will have a one-on-one interview dubbed 'An Insight, An Idea with Emmerson Mnangagwa'. It will come just moments before Europe's most powerful leader, Angela Merkel, presents her special address on the future of Europe.

For Mnangagwa, Davos presents an early opportunity to mix with the global elite and to showcase himself and his administration as he tries to forge new relationships following two decades of Zimbabwe's international isolation. The Mugabe regime was hugely unpopular and notorious for human rights violations, subversion of democracy and the rule of law. After decimating the institution of private property during the controversial land reform programme, Mugabe would have stuck out like a sore thumb in the neo-liberal environs of Davos.

Brief news was made by Patrick Zhuwao, who had remained outside the country since just before the fall of the Mugabe regime, when he threatened to confront Mnangagwa at the Forum in Davos. Nothing actually came of this, though, and Mnangagwa emerged from Davos with his head held high. From there, he flew to Addis Ababa, where his fellow African heads of state embraced him warmly and welcomed him into the African Union.

Unfortunately, this period of widespread optimism was soon followed by one of mourning. On 14 February 2018, Morgan Tsvangirai passed away while under treatment at a Johannesburg hospital. He was sixty-five years old. His death came three months to the day after the forced removal of President Mugabe, whom he had spent eighteen years battling to displace through democratic and peaceful means.

His burial in the rural Buhera District of Manicaland Province attracted a mammoth crowd, estimated by officials within the MDC-T to comprise around 400 000 people. But that figure is a more realistic estimate of the crowd that attended the open-air funeral service for Tsvangirai at Robert Mugabe Square in Harare.

Most news outlets reduced the number of attendees in Buhera to 'thousands'. However, given the number of buses supplied by the government, the MDC-T and various companies, as well as the volume of private vehicles that arrived for the burial, a reasonable figure for those who attended the burial in Buhera is somewhere between 60 000 and 70 000 people. This still makes it the largest gathering of mourners to attend the graveside of a fallen Zimbabwean hero since independence, alongside the National Heroes' Acre burial of Dr Joshua Nkomo in July 1999. It is even said to be the second-largest congregation of mourners ever to assemble on the African continent, exceeded in size only by the one for Nelson Mandela.

As Zimbabwe took steps towards its future, two of the country's leading academic luminaries – Dr Ibbo Mandaza, the director of the SAPES Trust, and Professor Jonathan Moyo, the former minister of higher and tertiary education – mounted platforms far away from Harare in order to caution their compatriots back home against accepting too readily the recent political developments.

Speaking at a seminar in Johannesburg on Zimbabwe's future, an event organised by the South African Institute of International Affairs, Mandaza reportedly said that the militarised ousting of President Mugabe had truly been a coup d'état. As such, it was important for the African Union, the European Union, the United States and Great Britain to recognise that the government now headed by Mnangagwa was an illegitimate or 'coup government'. Mandaza is known to prefer the idea of forming a transitional administration by bringing together elements from both the government and the various opposition parties.

He argued that the new government should 'not be allowed to get away with the transfer of power that happened' in November 2017. 'I wonder what would happen,' he said, 'if Mugabe were to leave for Singapore for his regular treatments. What if Mugabe, while out there, said he was forced to resign, which he was? What would be the implications? Can we explain why he is so closely guarded?'

As for Moyo, he was even more belligerent. After keeping hidden for over a month, during which time he was intermittently active on Twitter, Moyo suddenly appeared on the BBC programme *HARDtalk*, revealing that he had managed to escape from Zimbabwe with Kasukuwere before Mugabe was deposed and that they were taking refuge overseas. During Moyo's interview with Zeinab Badawi, who hosted the show, he came across as angry, nervous and rather insecure. His usual bluster and arrogance were significantly diminished in the shadow of recent events. Towards the end of the programme, Moyo sounded as though he might break into tears. Many who watched him that night later confessed that they felt genuine sympathy for him, despite the fact that he had ruined the careers of many Zimbabwean journalists in an effort to support President Mugabe.

Not long after, Moyo made another television appearance, this time for an interview on South Africa's SABC TV. He used this spotlight to insist that the people of Zimbabwe were disappointed that Mugabe had been removed from office. Many of the Zimbabweans whose opinions I personally canvassed were unhappy not only that Moyo appeared to be totally misinformed about the national mood but also that he was trying to mislead the international community in a desperate bid to undermine the new political order.

In reality, the general sentiment among Zimbabweans was that the new administration should be given a chance, especially if there was a guarantee of free and fair elections being held by the middle of 2018. Moyo seemed to be motivated more by his anger and frustration with the Mnangagwa administration than by any desire to positively influence the future of his home country.

However, more surprising than Moyo's defiant stance was the news that Joice Mujuru had paid a visit to the Blue Roof in February 2018. Far from pressing the matter of her husband's death, she reportedly used her meeting with the overthrown Mugabe to discuss a political reunion and strategy to fight against President Mnangagwa in the forthcoming elections.

Naturally, this alleged meeting astonished many Zimbabweans. Perhaps, though, such unpredictable politicking should be expected. After all, a lack of permanent factional alliances had always been part of ZANU-PF's intra-party conflicts. In his effort to hang on to power at all costs, Mugabe had often played his legitimately ambitious subordinates against each other, while portraying their ambitions as acts of disloyalty.

This strategy resulted in constantly changing political relationships. For example, while Jonathan Moyo had been a strategist for Mnangagwa at Tsholotsho in 2004 and a bitter enemy of the Mugabes, he had later become the First Family's chief strategist and an irreconcilable enemy of Mnangagwa's. And while Mnangagwa had cheered Grace Mugabe as she attacked Joice Mujuru in 2014, Mujuru had taken satisfaction three years later when Mnangagwa was fired as vice president and needed to flee Zimbabwe.

In the end, the greatest lesson to be learnt here is a salutary one: if the people of Zimbabwe are pushed against the wall by uncaring politicians, they will stand together and march against dictatorship and subjugation. It is a lesson that those bestowed with power now and in future should ignore at their own peril. This includes Mnangagwa, whose position at the helm of the new dispensation is still vulnerable to suffering a stillbirth at the 2018 harmonised elections owing to his long association with Mugabe. This opinion is particularly strong in opposition and youth circles.

As I was writing this chapter, there were reports in the media that Strive Masiyiwa, a famous London-based Zimbabwean business-person, was preparing to return home after eighteen years in self-imposed exile. He had locked horns with the Mugabe administration in the early 1990s during a battle to establish the now internationally acclaimed telecommunications group Econet Wireless, for which he serves as chief executive. Masiyiwa went on to become Zimbabwe's first US-dollar billionaire, despite the negative machinations of the Mugabe regime. In contrast to this extraordinary achievement is the reality that millions of his compatriots became instant Zimbabwe-dollar trillionaires at the height of the country's hyperinflation in 2008.

The Mnangagwa government is reported to have invited Masi-yiwa back from abroad, following the new president's appeal to Zimbabwean businesspeople in the diaspora to return home to help rebuild their country.

Although one swallow doesn't make a summer, the possibility that one of the country's most illustrious sons is returning to Zimbabwe inspires an encouraging view of the road ahead. There is optimism that the new dispensation, beyond ensuring free and fair elections in 2018, will be able to remedy the international isolation and economic hardships that have battered the country for nearly four decades as a result of Mugabe's dictatorship.

My completion of this chapter also coincided with the end of Mnangagwa's first 100 days in office. Overall, media reaction was quite mixed in judging his efforts and strategies during this period.

Zimbabwe's largest newspaper, *The Herald* – the flagship of Zimbabwe Newspapers, whose majority shareholder is the government – was positive about Mnangagwa's achievements. 'President Mnangagwa's first 100 days in office have been a huge success,' an article stated, 'with his administration setting the economy on a recovery trajectory.' Meanwhile, the UK-based *Zimbabwe Mail* was wholly dismissive. Under the headline 'Mnangagwa's 100 day target turns out another dumb squid', the newspaper opined: 'President Emmerson Mnangagwa clocks 100 days in office next week with his administration struggling to gain the confidence required to stem the cash crisis.'

Other publications offered a rather more balanced opinion. *NewsDay* published a somewhat sympathetic article, stating: 'President Emmerson Mnangagwa has appealed for patience as he winds up his first 100 days in office, saying, "It takes more than 100 days to recover an economy."'

In the meantime, the majority of Zimbabwe's citizens, especially those outside of active politics, have adopted a 'wait and see' attitude as the clock ticks towards the 2018 harmonised elections. Once again, ZANU-PF will be pitted against the MDC-T, although both parties are now without the particular leadership of Robert Mugabe and Morgan Tsvangirai. The outcome there will be an indication of the extent to which Mnangagwa has been absolved of the infamous legacy of his controversial predecessor, Robert Gabriel Mugabe.

Select Bibliography

Chikuhwa, Jacob W. *Zimbabwe: The End of the First Republic.*
   Bloomington, IN: AuthorHouse, 2013

Chung, Fay. *Re-Living the Second Chimurenga. Memories from
   Zimbabwe's Liberation Struggle.* Harare: Weaver Press, 2006

Copson, Raymond W. *Zimbabwe: Background and Issues.* New York:
   Nova Novinka; 2006

Hill, Geoff. *The Battle for Zimbabwe: The Final Countdown.*
   Cape Town: Zebra Press, 2003

Ian Smith. *The Great Betrayal.* London: Blake Publishing, 1997

Mario, Prince. *Zimbabwe, Land and the Dictator.* Morrisville, NC:
   Lulu Press, 2009

Meredith, Martin. *The State of Africa: A History of the Continent since
   Independence.* London: Simon & Schuster, 2013

Mitchell, Nancy. *Jimmy Carter in Africa, Race and the Cold War.*
   Palo Alto: Stanford University Press, 2016

Mukonori, Fidelis. *Man in the Middle: A Memoir.* Harare: The House
   of Books, 2018,

Ndlovu-Gatsheni, Sabelo J. (ed.). *Joshua Mqabuko Nkomo of Zimbabwe:
   Politics, Power, and Memory.* Basingstoke: Palgrave Macmillan, 2017

Nkomo, Joshua. *Nkomo: The Story of My Life.* Harare: Sapes Books, 2001

Sibanda, Eliakim M. *The Zimbabwe African People's Union, 1961-87:
   A Political History of Southern Africa.* Trenton, NJ: Africa World
   Press, 2005

Stiff, Peter. *Cry Zimbabwe.* Alberton: Galago, 2000

Thomson, Alex. *An Introduction to African Politics*. Abingdon: Routledge, 2010

Tsvangirai, Morgan. *At the Deep End*. Johannesburg: Penguin, 2011

White, Luise. *The Assassination of Herbert Chitepo: Texts and Politics in Zimbabwe*. Bloomington, IN: Indiana University Press; 2003

Index

ING